HOME DÉCOR
Sewing 101

CREATIVE PUBLISHING international

CHANHASSEN, MINNESOTA
www.creativepub.com

Copyright © 2004
Creative Publishing international, Inc.
18705 Lake Drive East
Chanhassen, Minnesota 55317
1-800-328-3895
www.creativepub.com

President/CEO: Michael Eleftheriou
Vice President/Publisher: Linda Ball
Vice President/Retail Sales: Kevin Haas

HOME DÉCOR SEWING 101

Created by: The Editors of Creative Publishing
international, Inc.

Executive Editor: Alison Brown Cerier
Managing Editor: Yen Le
Art Director: Lois Stanfield
Senior Editor: Linda Neubauer
Stylist: Joanne Wawra
Graphic Designer: Megan Noller
Photographer: Tate Carlson, John Abernathy
Director of Production: Kim Gerber
Production Manager: Laura Hokkanen

ISBN 1-58923-142-2

Library of Congress Cataloging-in-Publication Data

Home decor sewing 101 : a beginner's guide to sewing for the home / the
editors of Creative Publishing International, Inc.
      p. cm.
Includes index.
 ISBN 1-58923-142-2
 1. Household linens. 2. Machine sewing. 3. Textile fabrics in
interior decoration. I. Creative Publishing International. II. Title.
TT387.H668 2004
646.2'1--dc22

                                2003063475

Printed in Malaysia by:
 TWP SDN BHD
10 9 8 7 6 5 4 3 2 1

CONTENTS

How to Use This Book 4

Sewing Basics 6

Sewing Projects 40

Glossary & Index 174

How to USE THIS BOOK

Welcome to the rewarding world of sewing. *Home Décor Sewing 101* is designed to encourage creativity and instill confidence as you learn to sew. Easy-to-follow instructions with colorful photographs and illustrations help you build your sewing skills while making home decorating items that really appeal to you.

GLOSSARY TEXT

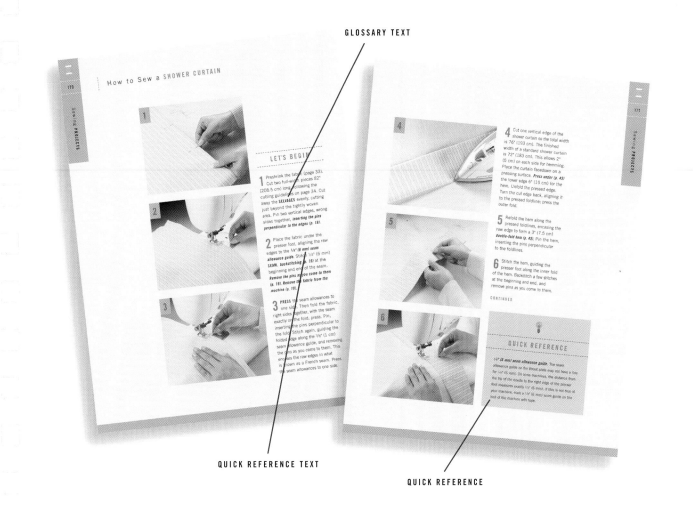

QUICK REFERENCE TEXT

QUICK REFERENCE

Sewing enthusiasts enjoy this time-honored art for many reasons. Home decorating items are popular projects for beginners and advanced sewers alike, partly because of the cost savings over purchased items. By sewing these items for the home, we also get to enjoy the creative fun of choosing styles, colors, and fabrics that fit our own personalities and tastes rather than those of the mass-produced market. But perhaps the greatest reason that sewing is so enjoyable is the mere satisfaction felt in creating something from scratch with your own two hands. Whether you are making something for your own home or to give to someone else, the ultimate reward is the intangible delight and personal fulfillment gained in the process.

The projects in this book are designed to guide you from your first nervous stitch at your sewing machine to comfortable familiarity. Each project will teach you new skills, listed under **What You'll Learn**. Throughout the book you will find tips and explanations to help you understand the "why" behind what you are doing. We also have included variations for the projects, encouraging you to explore the unlimited design and fabric possibilities.

Use the first section of the book to acquaint yourself with your sewing machine and the techniques and supplies that encompass the art of sewing. Your sewing machine owner's manual is a necessity; refer to it first if you have questions or problems specific to your machine.

The first step in any sewing project is to read through the directions from beginning to end. Refer to the **Quick References** at the right side of the pages for definitions or elaborations on any words or phrases printed *like this* on the page. If the word or phrase is followed by a page number, its reference can be found on the page indicated. Words printed **LIKE THIS** can be found in the **Glossary** that begins on page 174. At the beginning of every project you will find a list telling you **What You'll Need**. Read through the information on fabric before you go shopping, so the fabric store will seem a little more user-friendly when you get there.

Above all, enjoy the process. Give yourself the opportunity to be creative and express yourself through the things you sew.

Sewing BASICS

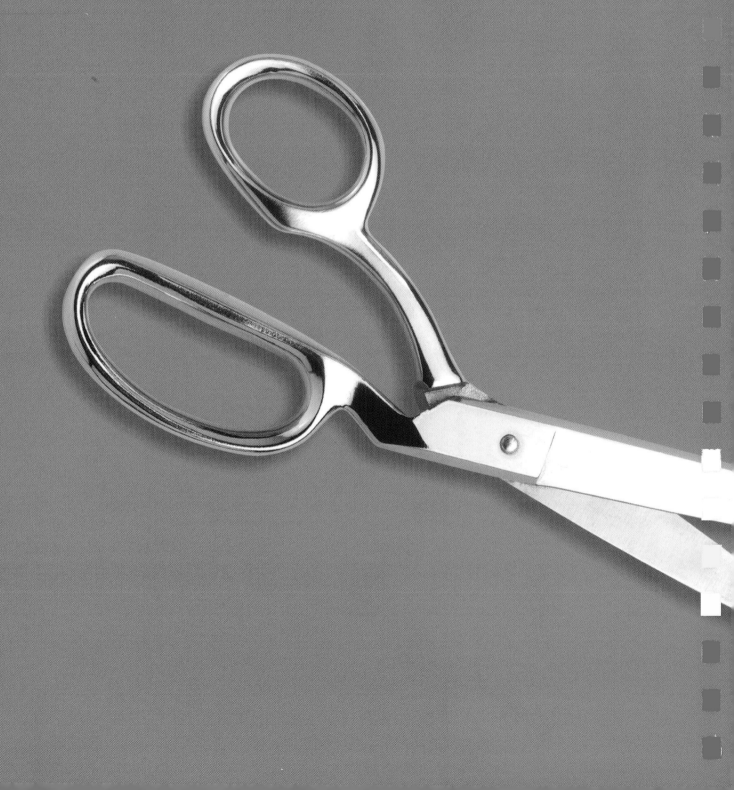

The Sewing Machine 8

Machine Accessories 10

Getting Ready to Sew 12

How to Balance Tension 16

Sewing a Seam 18

Sewing Supplies 20

Special Products 26

Fabric Information 30

Cutting Decorator Fabrics 34

Matching Designs 36

Hand Stitches 38

The Sewing MACHINE

The principle parts common to all modern sewing machines are shown in the diagrams at right. The parts may look different on your model, and they may have slightly different locations, so open your owner's manual, also. If you do not have an owner's manual for your machine, you should be able to get one from a sewing machine dealer who sells your brand. Become familiar with the names of the parts and their functions. As you spend more time sewing, these items will become second nature to you.

If you are buying a new machine, consider how much and what kind of sewing you expect to do. Talk to friends who sew and to sales personnel. Ask for demonstrations, and sew on the machine yourself. Experiment with the various features while sewing on a variety of fabrics, including knits, wovens, lightweights, and denim. Think about the optional features of the machine and which ones you want on yours. Many dealers offer free sewing lessons with the purchase of a machine. Take advantage! These lessons will be geared to your particular brand and model of sewing machine.

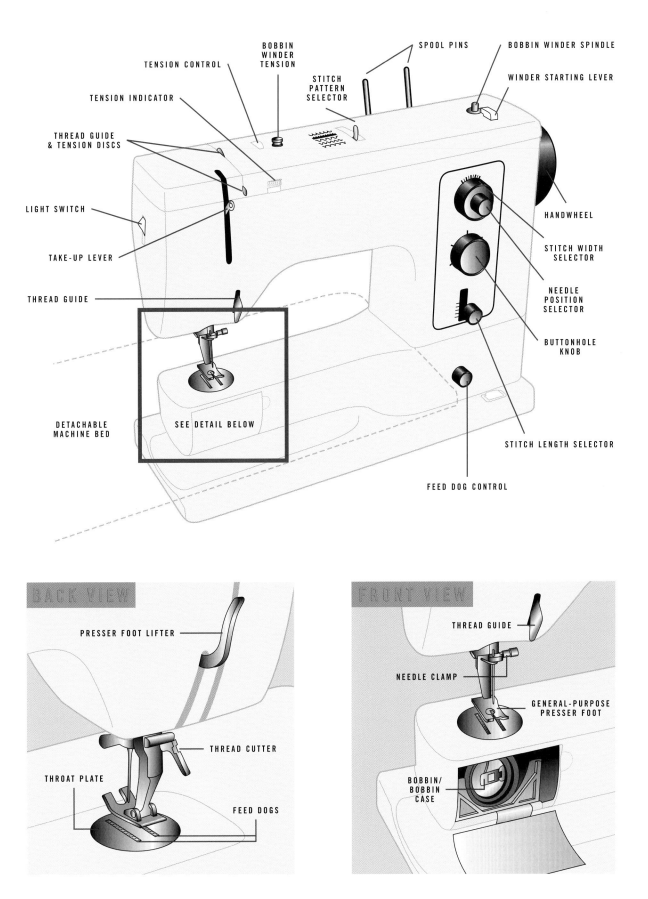

BOBBIN
WINDER
TENSION

TENSION CONTROL

TENSION INDICATOR

STITCH
PATTERN
SELECTOR

SPOOL PINS

BOBBIN WINDER SPINDLE

WINDER STARTING LEVER

THREAD GUIDE
& TENSION DISCS

LIGHT SWITCH

TAKE-UP LEVER

HANDWHEEL

STITCH WIDTH
SELECTOR

NEEDLE
POSITION
SELECTOR

THREAD GUIDE

BUTTONHOLE
KNOB

DETACHABLE
MACHINE BED

SEE DETAIL BELOW

STITCH LENGTH SELECTOR

FEED DOG CONTROL

BACK VIEW

PRESSER FOOT LIFTER

THREAD CUTTER

THROAT PLATE

FEED DOGS

FRONT VIEW

THREAD GUIDE

NEEDLE CLAMP

GENERAL-PURPOSE
PRESSER FOOT

BOBBIN/
BOBBIN
CASE

Machine ACCESSORIES

SEWING MACHINE NEEDLES

Sewing machine needles come in a variety of styles and sizes. The correct needle choice depends mostly on the fabric you have selected. Sharp points **(A)**, used for woven fabrics, are designed to pierce the fabric. Ballpoints **(B)** are designed to slip between the loops of knit fabric rather than pierce and possibly damage the fabric. Universal points **(C)** are designed to work on both woven and knitted fabrics. The size of the needle is designated by a number, generally given in both European (60, 70, 80, 90, 100, 110) and American (9, 11, 12, 14, 16, 18) numbering systems. Use size 11/70 or 12/80 needles for mediumweight fabrics. A larger number means the needle is thicker and that it is appropriate for use with heavier fabrics and heavier threads.

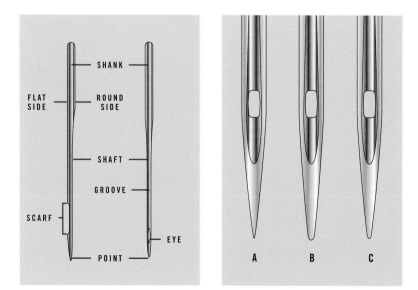

SHANK

FLAT SIDE   ROUND SIDE

SHAFT

GROOVE

SCARF

EYE

POINT

A   B   C

TIP Though needle style and size are usually indicated in some way on the needle, it is often difficult to see without a magnifying glass, and you most likely will not remember what needle is in the machine. As an easy reminder, when you finish a sewing session, leave a fabric swatch from your current project under the presser foot.

BOBBINS

Stitches are made by locking the upper thread with a lower thread, carried on a bobbin. Always use bobbins in the correct style and size for your machine. Bobbin thread tension is controlled by a spring on the bobbin case, which may be built in (A) or removable (B).

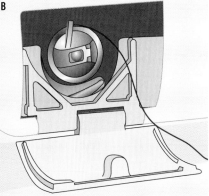

PRESSER FEET

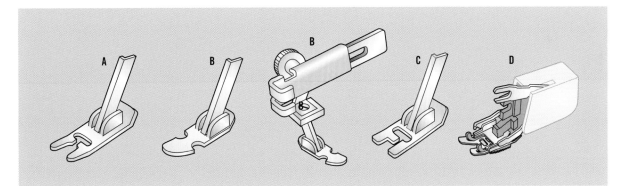

Every sewing machine comes with accessories for specialized tasks. More can be purchased as you develop your interest and skills. Your machine manual or dealer can show you what accessories are available and will explain how to use them to get the best results.

A general-purpose foot (A), probably the one you will use most often, has a wide opening to accommodate the side-to-side movement of the needle in all types of utility (nondecorative) stitches. It is also suitable for most straight stitching. A zipper foot (B) is used to insert zippers or to stitch any seam that has

more bulk on one side than the other. For some sewing machines, the zipper foot is stationary, requiring you to move the needle position to the right or left. For other styles, the position of the zipper foot itself is adjustable. A special-purpose or embroidery foot (C) has a grooved bottom that allows the foot to ride smoothly over decorative stitches or raised cords. Some styles are clear plastic, allowing you to see your work more clearly. A walking foot (D) feeds top and bottom layers at equal rates, allowing you to more easily match patterns or stitch bulky layers, as in quilted projects.

Getting Ready to SEW

Simple tasks of inserting the needle, winding the bobbin, and threading the machine have tremendous influence on the stitch quality and performance of your machine. Use this guide as a general reference, but refer to your owner's manual for instructions specific to your machine.

INSERTING THE NEEDLE

Loosen the needle clamp. After selecting the appropriate needle for your project (page 10), insert it into the machine as high as it will go. The grooved side of the needle faces forward if your bobbin gets inserted from the front or top; it faces to the left if your bobbin gets inserted on the left. Tighten the clamp securely.

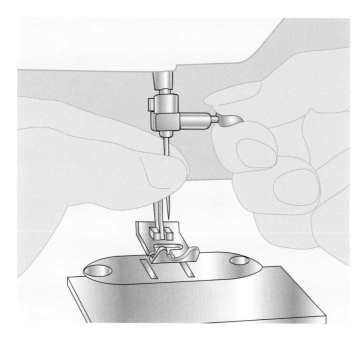

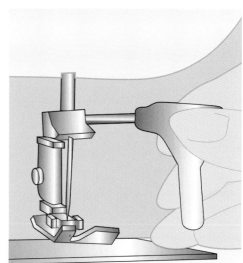

WINDING THE BOBBIN

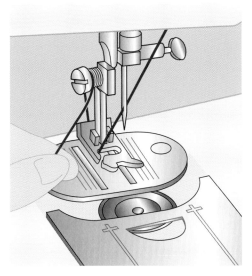

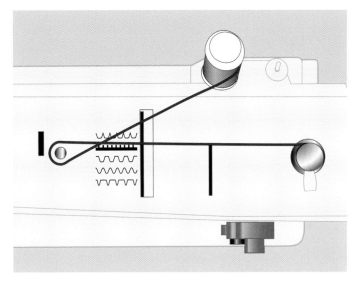

If the bobbin case is built in, the bobbin is wound in place with the machine fully threaded as if to sew (page 14).

Removable bobbins are wound on the top or side of the machine, with the machine threaded for bobbin winding, as described in your owner's manual.

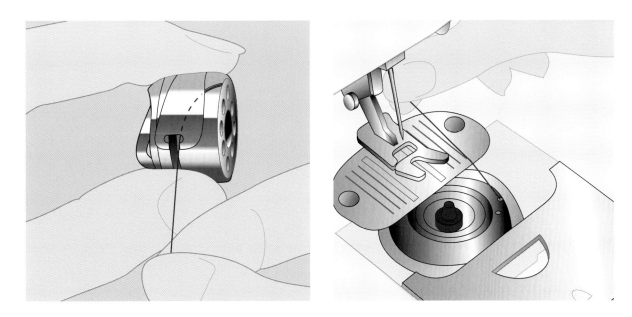

Bobbin thread must be drawn through the bobbin case tension spring. For wind-in-place bobbins, this happens automatically when you wind the bobbin, but you must do it manually when you insert a bobbin that already has thread on it.

THREADING THE MACHINE

Because every sewing machine is different, the threading procedure for your machine may differ slightly from the one shown here. Once again, it is important to refer to your owner's manual. Every upper thread guide adds a little tension to the thread as it winds its way to the needle. Missing one of them can make a big difference in the quality of your stitches.

1 Set the thread spool on the spindle.

A. Vertical spindle. Position the spool so that it will turn clockwise as you sew.

B. Horizontal spindle. The spool is held in place with an end cap. If your spool has a small cut in one end for minding the thread, position the spool with that end to the right.

> TIP — If the spool is new and has paper labels covering the holes, poke them in, completely uncovering the holes, to allow the spool to turn freely.

Unless your machine has a self-winding bobbin, you will want to wind the bobbin (page 13) before threading the machine.

2 Pull thread to the left and through the first thread guide.

3 Draw thread through the tension guide.

> TIP — It is very important to have the presser foot lever up when threading the machine because the tension discs are then open. If the presser foot is down and the discs are closed, the thread will not slide between the discs, and your stitches will not make you happy.

4 Draw thread through the next thread guide.

5 Insert thread through the take-up lever.

6 Draw the thread through the remaining thread guides.

7 Thread the needle. Most needles are threaded from front to back; some, from left to right.

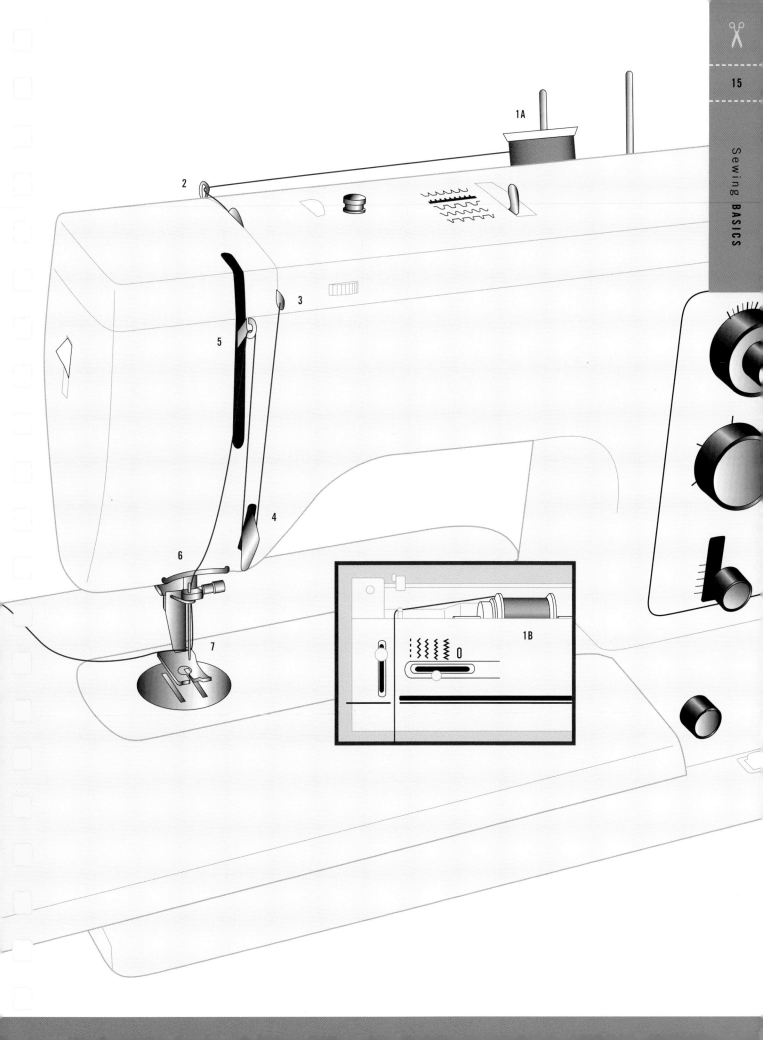

How to BALANCE TENSION

Your machine forms stitches by interlocking the bobbin thread with the needle thread. Every time the needle goes down into the fabric, a sharp hook catches the needle thread and wraps the bobbin thread around it. Imagine this little tug of war. If the needle thread tension is "stronger" than the bobbin thread tension, the needle thread pulls the bobbin thread through to the top. If the bobbin thread tension is "stronger," it pulls the needle thread through to the bottom. When the tensions are evenly balanced, the stitch will lock exactly halfway between the top and bottom of the layers being sewn, which is right where you want it.

Some machines have "self-adjusting tension," meaning the machine automatically adjusts its tension with every fabric you sew. For machines that do not have this feature, you may have to adjust the needle thread tension slightly as you sew different fabrics.

TESTING THE TENSION

1 Thread your machine and insert the bobbin, using two very different colors of thread, neither of which matches the fabric. Cut an 8" (20.5 cm) square of a smooth, mediumweight fabric. Fold the fabric in half diagonally, and place it under the presser foot so the fold aligns to your 1/2" (1.3 cm) seam guide. Lower the presser foot and set your stitch length at 10 stitches per inch or 2.5 mm long.

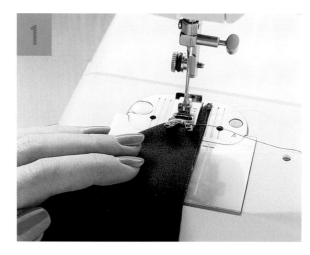

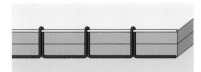

Top tension too tight

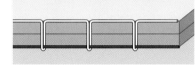

Top tension too loose

Tensions even

2 Stitch a line across the fabric, stitching ½" (1.3 cm) from the diagonal fold. Remove the fabric from the machine. Inspect your stitching line from both sides. If your tension is evenly balanced, you will see only one color on each side. If you see both thread colors on the top side of your sample, the needle tension is tighter than the bobbin tension. If you see both thread colors on the back side of your sample, the bobbin tension is tighter than the needle tension.

3 Pull on your stitching line until you hear threads break. (Because you stitched on the **BIAS**, the fabric will stretch slightly.) If the thread breaks on only one side, your machine's tension is tighter on that side.

ADJUSTING THE TENSION

Before adjusting the tension on your machine, first check:
• that your machine is properly threaded (page 14)
• that your bobbin is properly installed
• that your needle is not damaged and is inserted correctly.

After checking these three things, you may need to adjust the tension on your machine. (Check your owner's manual.) Tighten or loosen the needle thread tension slightly to bring the needle thread and bobbin thread tensions into balance. Test the stitches after each adjustment until you achieve balanced tension. If slight adjustments of the needle tension dial do not solve the problem, the bobbin tension may need adjusting. However, most manufacturers do not recommend that you adjust bobbin tension yourself, so unless you have received instructions for your machine, take your machine in for repair.

Sewing a SEAM

Y ou may or may not be familiar with the very basic technique of running your machine and sewing a seam. Use this exercise as a refresher course whenever you feel you have lost touch with the basics or if your personal technique has become sloppy. Little frustrations, such as thread jams, erratic stitching lines, or having the thread pull out of the needle at the start of a seam, can often be prevented or corrected by following these basic guidelines. If you are really not sure where to begin, then you should probably begin right here!

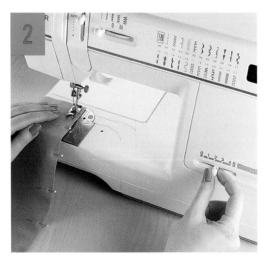

1 Thread your machine (page 14) and insert the bobbin (page 13). Holding the needle thread with your left hand, turn the handwheel toward you until the needle has gone down and come back up to its highest point. A stitch will form, and you will feel a tug on the needle thread. Pull on the needle thread to bring the bobbin thread up through the hole in the throat plate. Pull both threads together under the presser foot and off to one side.

2 Cut two pieces of fabric and place them right sides together, aligning the outer edges. Pin the pieces together along one long edge, *inserting the pins* about every 2" (5 cm), *perpendicular to the edge.* Place the fabric under the presser foot so the pinned side edges align to the 1/2" (1.3 cm) *seam allowance guide* and the upper edges are just behind the opening of the presser foot. Lower the presser foot, and set your stitch length at 2.5 mm, which equals 10 stitches per inch.

3 Begin by *backstitching* several stitches to the upper edge of the fabric. Hold the thread tails under a finger for the first few stitches. This prevents the needle thread from being pulled out of the needle and also prevents the thread tails from being drawn down into the bobbin case, where they could potentially cause the dreaded **THREAD JAM**.

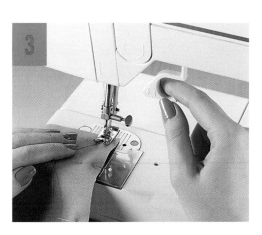

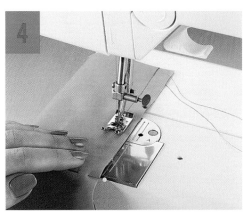

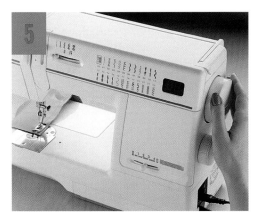

Inserting the pins perpendicular to the edge. In this position, the pin heads are near the raw edge where you can easily grasp them with your right hand. You are also much less likely to stick yourself with a pin as you sew.

Seam allowance guide. Most machines have a series of lines on the throat plate. These lines mark the distance from the needle (where a standard straight stitch seam would be) to the cut edges. Measure these lines on your machine to determine where the edge of your fabric should be for the width seam you are stitching.

Backstitching keeps the beginning and end of your stitching line from pulling out. Check your owner's manual to see how to backstitch with your machine. You may need to lift and hold your stitch length lever, push in and hold a button, or simply touch an icon.

Remove pins as you come to them. As tempting as it may be, don't sew over pins! You may be lucky and save a few seconds, or you could hit a pin and break the needle.

Remove the fabric from the machine. Pull the fabric smoothly away from the presser foot, either to the left side or straight back. If you have to tug the threads, turn your handwheel slightly toward you until they pull easily. Cut the threads, leaving tails 2½" to 3" (6.5 to 7.5 cm) long.

4 Stitch forward over the backstitched line, and continue sewing the ½" (1.3 cm) seam. Gently guide the fabric while you sew by walking your fingers ahead of and slightly to the sides of the presser foot. Remember, you are only guiding; let the machine pull the fabric.

5 Stop stitching and *remove pins as you come to them.* When you reach the end of the fabric, stop stitching; backstitch several stitches, and stop again. Turn the handwheel toward you until the needle is in its highest position.

6 Raise the presser foot. *Remove the fabric from the machine.*

Sewing SUPPLIES

I n the process of sewing home décor items, you will need various tools

and supplies for measuring, marking, cutting, sewing, and pressing. You

may already own some of these tools and supplies, but don't feel that

you must get them all before you start sewing. You will undoubtedly acquire

tools as your sewing skills and interest grow.

PINS AND HAND-SEWING SUPPLIES

Pins are available in a variety of sizes and styles. Look for rustproof pins and needles made of brass, nickel-plated steel, or stainless steel. Pictured from top to bottom:

Straight pins. Select long sturdy pins with large plastic heads to make them highly visible and easy to remove.

T-pins, used by most professional drapery workrooms, are another good choice.

Sharps are all-purpose, medium-length needles designed for general hand-sewing tasks.

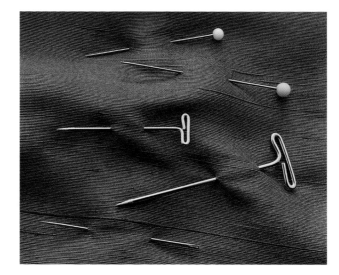

A Pincushion provides a safe and handy place to store pins. Some pin-cushions are magnetic so the pins won't spill. Be sure not to place any magnetic tools near a computerized machine, as the magnet can play havoc with the machine's memory.

B Thimble protects your finger while hand sewing. Available in a variety of styles and sizes, it is worn on whichever finger you use to push the needle through the fabric. Most people prefer either the middle or ring finger. Using a thimble is an acquired habit. Some people can't get along without it while others can never get used to it.

C Needle threader eases threading of hand and machine needles. These are especially useful if you have difficulty seeing something that small.

D Beeswax with holder strengthens thread and prevents tangling while hand sewing.

MEASURING AND MARKING TOOLS

A Transparent ruler allows you to see what you are measuring and marking. It also is used to check fabric grainline.

B Yardstick (meterstick) should be made of smooth hardwood or metal.

C Tape measure has the flexibility helpful for measuring items with shape and dimension. Select one made of a material that will not stretch.

D Seam gauge is a 6" (15 cm) metal or plastic ruler with a sliding marker. It helps make quick, accurate measurements and can be used to measure seam allowance widths.

E Transparent T-square is used to locate grainlines and to measure 90-degree angles.

F Marking chalk is available in several forms; as powder in a rolling wheel dispenser, as a pencil, or as a flat slice. Chalk lines are easily removable from most fabrics.

G Fabric marking pens are available in both air-erasable and water-erasable forms. Air-erasable marks disappear in 48 hours; water-erasable marks wash off with a sprinkling of water.

H Narrow masking tape is an alternative method for marking fabrics when other methods are less suitable.

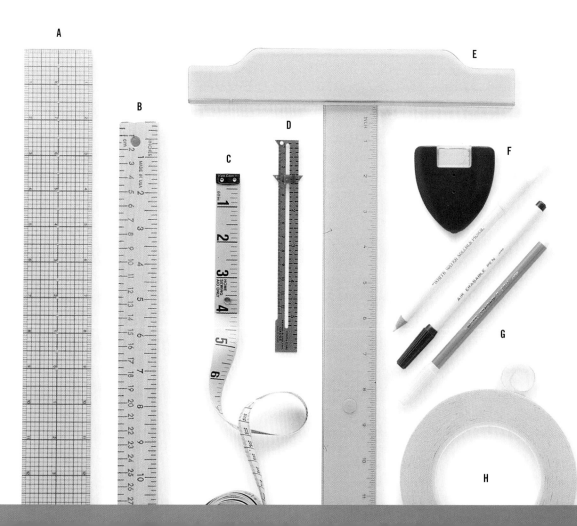

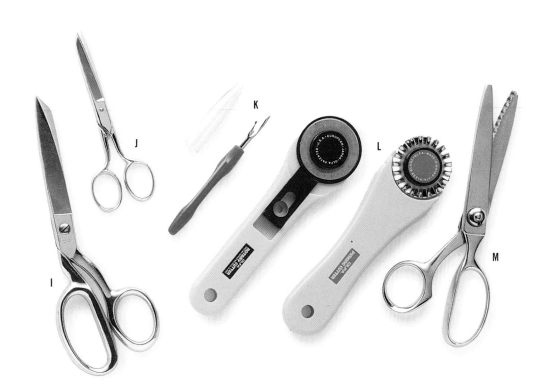

CUTTING TOOLS

Buy quality cutting tools and use them only for your sewing! Cutting paper or other household materials will dull your cutting tools quickly. Dull tools are not only tiresome to work with, they can also damage fabric. Scissors have both handles the same size; shears have one handle larger than the other. The best-quality scissors and shears are hot-forged, high-grade steel, honed to a fine cutting edge. Blades should be joined with an adjustable screw to ensure even pressure along the length of the blade. Have your cutting tools sharpened periodically by a qualified professional.

I Bent-handled dressmaker's shears are best for cutting fabric shapes because the angle of the lower blade lets fabric lie flat on the cutting surface. Blade lengths of 7" or 8" (18 or 20.5 cm) are most popular, but lengths of up to 12" (30.5 cm) are available. Select a blade length appropriate for the size of your hand—shorter lengths for smaller hands. Left-handed models are also available. If you intend to sew a great deal, invest in a pair of all-steel, chrome-plated shears for heavy-duty cutting. Lighter models with stainless steel blades and plastic handles are fine for less-frequent sewing or lightweight fabrics.

J Sewing scissors have one pointed and one rounded tip for clipping threads and trimming and clipping seam allowances. A 6" (15 cm) blade is suitable for most tasks.

K Seam ripper quickly removes stitches and opens buttonholes. Use it carefully to avoid cutting the fabric.

L Rotary cutter works like a pizza cutter and can be used by left-handed or right-handed sewers. A locking mechanism retracts the blade for safety. Use the rotary cutter with a special plastic mat available in different sizes, with or without grid lines. The self-healing mat protects both the work surface and the blade.

M Pinking shears and **pinking rotary cutters** are used to finish seams. They cut fabric in a zigzag or scalloped pattern instead of a straight line.

PRESSING TOOLS AND MORE

PRESSING as you sew is one important procedure that should not be neglected. It may seem like a needless interruption, but pressing at each stage of construction is the secret to a perfectly finished project. The general rule is to press each **SEAM** before crossing it with another.

A Steam/spray iron should have a wide temperature range to accommodate all fabrics. Buy a dependable, name-brand iron. An iron that steams and sprays at any setting, not just the higher heat settings, is helpful for fabrics with synthetic fibers.

B Seam roll is a firmly packed cylindrical cushion for pressing seams. A heavy cardboard tube works well, too. The fabric falls to the sides away from the iron, preventing the **SEAM ALLOWANCES** from making an imprint on the right side of the fabric.

C Point turner, made of wood or plastic, safely pokes out stitched corners on items like pillows and placemats. The rounded end allows you to hold seam allowances open for pressing without getting your fingers too close to the iron.

D Glues can be used instead of pins to hold trims or decorative motifs in place for stitching. Water-soluble adhesives, such as glue sticks, provide only a temporary bond. Liquid fabric glues can be dotted between layers to join them. Look for glues that dry clear and flexible.

E Liquid fray preventer is a colorless plastic liquid that prevents fraying by stiffening the fabric slightly. It is helpful when you have clipped too far into a seam allowance or want to prevent the cut end of a decorative trim from fraying. It may darken some colors, so test before using and apply carefully. The liquid may be removed with rubbing alcohol, but it dries to a permanent finish that withstands laundering and dry cleaning.

F Cutting boards protect a table's finish from scratches. Available in padded style, cardboard, or plastic, the board provides a wide flat surface for rolling out the fabric, marking, and cutting. This padded style can also be used for pressing.

G Press cloth helps prevent iron shine. The transparent variety allows you to see if the fabric is smooth and properly aligned.

H Teflon-coated sole plate guard, available to fit most irons, eliminates the need for a press cloth.

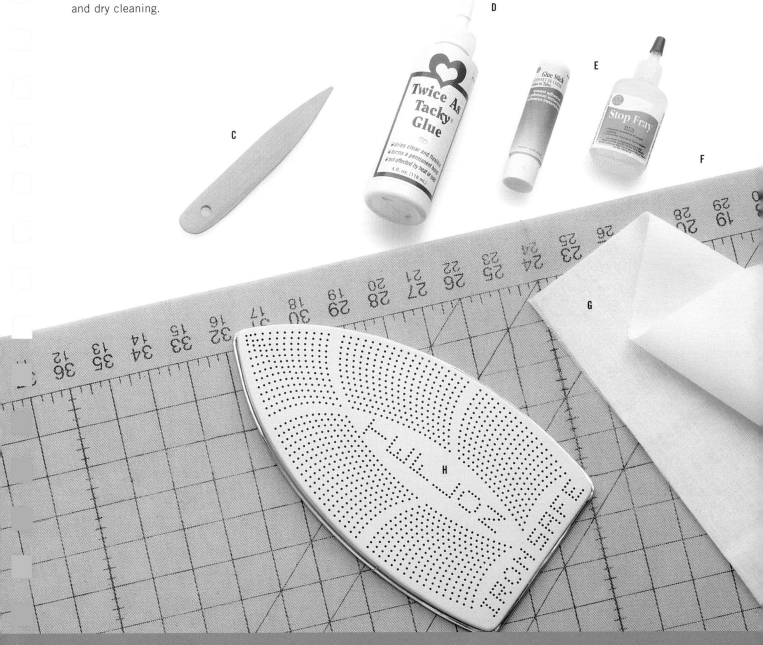

Special PRODUCTS

Many special products and gadgets are designed to assist you in various steps of the sewing process. Before using a new product, read the manufacturer's instructions carefully. Learn what special handling or care is required, and for what fabrics or sewing techniques it is especially suited. Here are some specialized products, available in fabric stores, that you may find helpful in sewing your home décor items.

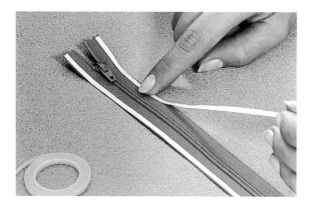

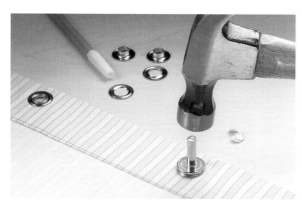

Basting tape is double-faced adhesive tape used instead of pinning or basting. It is especially helpful for matching prints, applying zippers, and positioning trims. Some manufacturers advise that you avoid stitching through the tape because the adhesive may collect on your needle.

Paper-backed fusible web is sold on rolls, in various narrow widths. It is also available as a wide sheet rolled on a bolt for purchase by the yard (meter). It is a timesaving product used for adhering two pieces of fabric together. For instance, you may use a narrow strip of fusible web to close the opening in a window topper. A protective paper backing is removed from one side after the other side has been fused to the fabric.

Grommets make reinforced holes in fabric for items such as shower curtains. They are available in different sizes, in silver or brass finish. The manufacturer also makes special tools for punching holes and installing the grommets. The tools are sold separately, so you don't have to buy them each time you buy grommets.

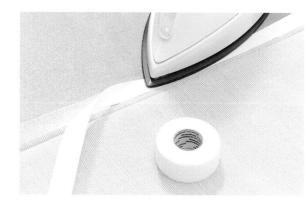

Welting is a fabric-covered cording, sewn into a seam or around an outer edge to provide extra strength and a decorative finishing touch. It is available in many colors and various diameters to purchase by the yard (meter) or in precut packaged lengths.

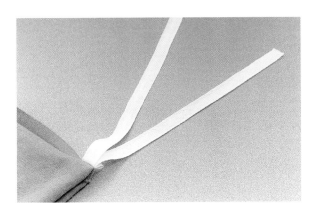

Twill tape is a sturdy nondecorative fabric strip that has many sewing uses. For instance, lengths of twill tape are sewn at the corners inside the duvet cover for tying the duvet in place, a convenient feature rarely found in ready-made bedding. Packaged white twill tape is available in a choice of narrow widths.

Batting. Low-loft cotton, polyester, or poly/cotton blend batting, sold in packages, is used for quilted projects, such as channel-quilted placemats. It is soft and drapable. Polyester upholstery batting, used for button-tufted cushions, is a firm, crisp batting with high loft, usually sold by the yard (meter) from a large roll.

CONTINUED

Buttons for covering are available in kits, complete with a button front and back and the tools for covering the button. Dampen the fabric to make it easier to handle. The fabric may shrink slightly as it dries to fit more smoothly around the button. Use the eraser end of a pencil to secure the fabric to the prongs of the button front, working back and forth across the button to tuck all the fabric into the button front.

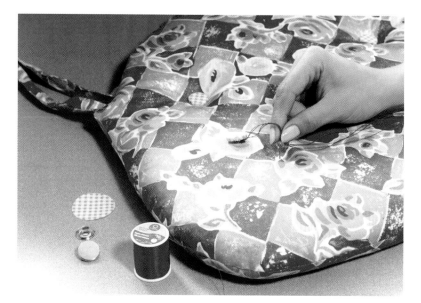

Button and carpet thread is a strong, heavy thread recommended for hand sewing when long-term durability is necessary, such as button-tufting a cushion. The thread has a polyester core wrapped with cotton. A polished glacé finish prevents thread abrasion and tangling.

Zippers come in a wide range of styles for many different uses. For the zipper closure on a pillow, choose a conventional polyester coil zipper (not a separating style) in a color to match your fabric.

Flat decorator trims and grosgrain ribbons can be machine-sewn to some items, such as decorator pillows, for a designer touch. Bulkier trims can be stitched on by hand.

Polyurethane foam can be purchased at most fabric stores that have home decorating areas or from specialty foam stores. It is available in various thicknesses, densities, and widths. The store will usually cut foam to the size you need, or you can cut thinner foam yourself using sewing shears, a serrated knife, or an electric knife.

Pillow forms offer you the convenience of being able to "stuff" and "unstuff" your pillow quickly and neatly. Inexpensive forms, stuffed with generous amounts of polyester fiberfill, are available in a range of rectangular and round sizes. For extra softness and luxury, you may want to pay the higher price for down-filled pillow forms.

Fabric INFORMATION

The creative fun begins with choosing the fabrics for your home décor projects. Aside from knowing you want a certain color or a printed pattern, there are other decisions to make. Do you need a fabric that can be laundered frequently? Are features such as wrinkle resistance and stain resistance important? Do you want smooth or textured, stiff or drapable, lightweight or heavy? Some basic fabric knowledge and a thought-out plan will help you make wise choices and avoid costly errors.

TYPES OF FABRICS

Natural fabrics are made from plant or animal fibers, spun into yarns; cotton, wool, silk, and linen are the most common. Naturals are often considered the easiest fabrics to sew. Synthetic fabrics, made from chemically produced fibers, include nylon, acrylic, acetate, and polyester. Rayon is a manmade fiber derived from a plant source. Each fiber has unique characteristics, desirable for different reasons. Many fabrics are a blend of natural and synthetic fibers, offering you the best qualities of each, such as the breathable comfort of cotton blended with the wrinkle resistance of polyester.

Most fabrics suitable for home décor are woven, having straight lengthwise and crosswise yarns. The pattern in which the yarns are woven gives the fabric its characteristic surface texture and appearance. The firmly woven outer edges of woven fabrics are called **SELVAGES**. As a general rule, the selvages should be trimmed away because they will shrink when they are pressed and cause seams to pucker. Strong, stable lengthwise yarns, running parallel to the selvages, form the **LENGTHWISE GRAIN**. The **CROSSWISE GRAIN** is perpendicular to the lengthwise grain and has a small amount of give. Any diagonal direction, called the **BIAS**, has a fair amount of stretch.

-DRY CLEANING RECOMMEND

WIDTH - 60" (152.5 CM)
MACHINE WASH
COTTON/25% POLYESTER

SHOPPING

Fabrics in a store are divided into fashion fabrics and decorator fabrics. Decorator fabrics are generally more durable than fashion fabrics; most have stain-resistant finishes. For this reason, it is often recommended that decorator fabrics be dry-cleaned rather than laundered. Manufactured in widths of 48" or 54" (122 or 137 cm), they are designed for pillows, window treatments, and other home decorating projects. One advantage of decorator fabrics is that they often are manufactured in groups of coordinating colors and designs so you can mix and match fabrics for a foolproof scheme. To prevent creases, decorator fabrics are rolled on cardboard tubes.

The designs in patterned decorator fabrics repeat vertically at regular intervals and, when fabric widths are sewn together, flow uninterrupted across the **SEAM**, making seams less noticeable. This is usually not true of patterned fashion fabrics. This **PATTERN REPEAT** is indicated on the **FABRIC IDENTIFICATION LABEL** and is essential for determining the amount of fabric you need.

Fashion fabrics are usually folded double and rolled on cardboard bolts. The most common widths are 36", 45", and 60" (91.5, 115, and 152.5 cm). Though fashion fabrics are intended for apparel, many are suitable for home décor items, especially when you want washable fabrics.

FABRIC PREPARATION

PRESHRINK any dry-clean-only fabrics by steaming. Move the iron evenly along the grainlines, hovering just above the surface of the fabric. Allow the fabric to dry before moving it. Preshrink washable fabrics by washing and drying in the same way you intend to care for the finished item.

Cutting DECORATOR FABRICS

C utting into a new piece of fabric may seem a little scary, considering the investment you have just made. Here are a few guidelines for accurate cutting that should boost your confidence.

After preshrinking, straighten the cut ends of the fabric, using one of the three methods opposite. Then mark the other cutting lines, using the straightened edge as a guide. Before cutting full-width pieces of fabric for large home décor projects, such as tablecloths, window swags, or rod-pocket curtains, pin-mark the placement of each cut along the **SELVAGE**. Mark out pieces for smaller projects, such as decorator pillows or napkins, with chalk. Double-check your measurements and inspect the fabric for flaws. Once you have cut into the fabric, you cannot return it. To ensure that large décor items will hang or lay straight, the fabric lengths must be cut on-grain. This means that the cuts are made along the exact **CROSSWISE GRAIN** of the fabric. Patterned decorator fabrics are cut following the **PATTERN REPEAT** rather than the grainline so they must be *printed on-grain*.

For tightly woven fabrics without a matchable pattern, mark straight cuts on the crosswise grain, using a carpenter's square. Align one edge to a selvage and mark along the perpendicular side.

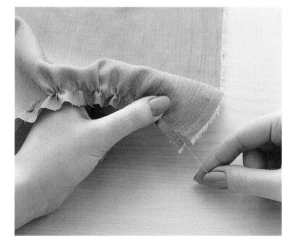

For loosely woven fabrics, such as linen tablecloth fabric, pull out a yarn along the crosswise grain, from selvage to selvage. Cut along the line left by the missing yarn.

QUICK REFERENCE

Printed on-grain. This means the pattern repeat coincides exactly with the crosswise grain of the fabric. To test fabric before you buy, place it on a flat surface and fold the cut edge back, aligning the selvages on the sides. Crease the fold with your fingers, then unfold the fabric and check to see if the crease runs into the selvage at exactly the same point in the pattern on both sides. Slight differences of less than 2" (5 cm) can usually be corrected by stretching the fabric diagonally. Avoid buying fabric that is printed more that 2" (5 cm) off-grain, as you will not be able to correct it, and the finished project will not hang straight.

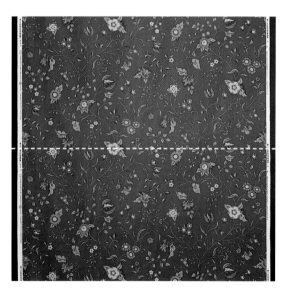

For tightly woven patterned decorator fabric, mark both selvages at the exact same point in the pattern repeat. Using a long straightedge, draw a line connecting the two points. If you will be stitching two or more full widths of fabric together, make all the cuts at the same location in the repeat. This usually means that you cut the pieces longer than necessary, stitch them together, and then trim them to the necessary length.

Matching DESIGNS

Stitching **SEAMS** in printed fabrics and fabrics with woven-in patterns requires a few extra steps to make sure the pattern will flow uninterrupted from one fabric width to the next.

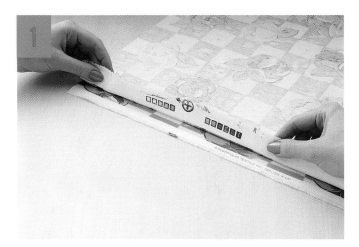

1 Place two fabric widths right sides together, aligning the **SELVAGES**. Fold back the upper selvage until the pattern matches. Adjust the top layer slightly up or down so that the pattern lines up exactly. **PRESS** the foldline.

2 Unfold the pressed selvage, and pin the fabric widths together, inserting the pins in and parallel to the foldline.

3 Turn the fabric over, and check the match from the right side. Make any necessary adjustments.

4 Repin the fabric so the pins are perpendicular to the foldline. Stitch the seam following the foldline; remove the pins as you come to them.

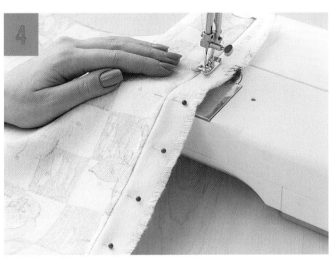

5 Check the match from the right side again. Make any necessary adjustments. Trim away the selvages, cutting the **SEAM ALLOWANCES** to 1/2" (1.3 cm).

6 Trim the entire fabric panel to the necessary **CUT LENGTH** as determined in the project instructions. (Remember your initial cut length for the patterned fabric included extra length to accommodate the **PATTERN REPEAT**.)

Hand STITCHES

While modern sewers rely on sewing machines for speedy construction, there are situations when hand stitching is necessary or preferable. You may need to slipstitch an opening closed in a pillow or button-tufted cushion. Of course, you'll also need to sew on buttons.

THREADING THE NEEDLE

Insert the thread end through the needle's eye, for sewing with a single strand. Or fold the thread in half, and insert the fold through the eye, for sewing with a double strand. Pull through about 8" (20.5 cm). Wrap the other end(s) around your index finger. Then, using your thumb, roll the thread off your finger, twisting it into a knot.

TIP Use a single strand when slipstitching or hemming. Use a double strand when sewing on buttons. To avoid tangles, begin with thread no longer than 18" (46 cm) from the needle to the knot. Run the thread through beeswax (page 21), if desired.

SLIPSTITCHING

1 Insert the threaded needle between the seam allowance and the outer fabric, just behind the opening. Bring it to the outside in the seamline. If you are right-handed, work from right to left; lefties work from left to right.

2 Insert the needle into the fold just behind where the thread came up, and run it inside the fold for about ¼" (6 mm). Bring the needle out, and draw the thread snug. Take your next stitch in the opposite fold, inserting the needle directly across from the previous stitch.

3 Continue, crossing from one fold to the other, until you have sewn past the opening. Secure the thread with several tiny stitches in the seamline. Then take a long stitch, and pull it tight. Clip the thread at the surface, and let the tail disappear inside.

SEWING ON A SHANK BUTTON

  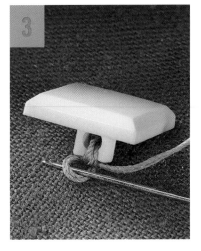

1 Place the button on the mark, with the shank hole parallel to the buttonhole. Secure the thread on the right side of the fabric with a small stitch under the button.

2 Bring the needle through the shank hole. Insert the needle down through the fabric and pull the thread through. Take four to six stitches in this manner.

3 Secure the thread in the fabric under the button by making a knot or by taking several small stitches. Clip the thread ends.

SEWING ON A SEW-THROUGH BUTTON

1 Place the button on the mark, with the holes lining up parallel to the buttonhole. Bring the needle through the fabric from the underside and up through one hole in the button. Insert the needle into another hole and through the fabric layers.

2 Slip a toothpick, match, or sewing machine needle between the thread and the button to form a shank. Take three or four stitches through each pair of holes. Bring the needle and thread to the right side under the button. Remove the toothpick.

3 Wind the thread two or three times around the button stitches to form the shank. Secure the thread on the right side under the button, by making a knot or taking several small stitches. Clip the threads close to the knot.

Sewing PROJECTS

Scarf Swags 43

Self-lined Rectangle Valance 47

Strap-tied Valance 53

Window Topper 63

Relaxed Rod-pocket Curtains 73

Placemats and Napkins 79

Banded Tablecloth 87

Button-tufted Cushion 95

Reversible Seat Covers 105

Synthetic Fleece Throw 111

Knife-edge Pillows 115

Nine-patch Pillows 123

Harem Pillows 127

Mock-box Pillows 131

Decorator Pillows 135

Envelope Pillows 143

Pillow Cases 149

Flanged Pillow Shams 155

Duvet Cover 161

Shower Curtain 169

Scarf SWAGS

This elegant and versatile window treatment actually requires very little sewing at all. A scarf swag is simply a long length of fabric that is **HEMMED** at the ends. If the fabric **SELVAGES** are neat and unpuckered, they can be left intact to serve as finished edges for the long sides of the swag. If they are unsightly, the selvages can be trimmed off and hemmed with the same technique used on the ends. The keys to success are making the swag to the right measurement and styling it over the window for a decorator look. You will use the entire width of a decorator fabric, running the **LENGTHWISE GRAIN** up one side, draping across the rod, and down the opposite side. Avoid **DIRECTIONAL PRINTS**, such as birds or flowers that only look right in one direction—you don't want to have birds flying upside down or tulips standing on their heads on one side of your window.

WHAT YOU'LL LEARN

How to measure a window for a swag

How to sew double-fold hems

How to style a swag over a window

Making a decorator window treatment is easier than you thought!

WHAT YOU'LL NEED

Decorative curtain rod and mounting hardware

Long cord or string and tape measure for determining length

Nondirectional decorator fabric in the amount determined in step 1

Thread to match the fabric

How to Sew a SCARF SWAG

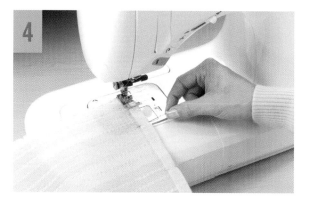

1 Mount the rod above the window frame, with the outer brackets beyond the frame sides. To determine the fabric length needed, drape a cord in the path you want the lower edge of the swag to follow. Cut the fabric 2" (5 cm) longer than this length, following the cutting directions on page 34.

2 *Press under* 1" (2.5 cm) on one end of the swag panel. Unfold the pressed edge. Turn the cut edge back, aligning it to the first foldline; press the outer fold.

3 Refold the edge along the pressed foldlines, encasing the raw edge to form a 1/2" (1.3 cm) *double-fold hem.* Pin the hem, *inserting the pins perpendicular to the folds (p. 19).*

4 Place the pinned hem under the presser foot of the machine, with the wrong side of the panel facing up. The bulk of the fabric will be to the left of the machine. The selvage edge should be under the presser foot, with the needle aligned to enter the fabric just inside the inner fold.

5 *Backstitch (p. 19)* along the inner fold to the selvage. Reverse the direction and stitch forward, stitching the entire length of the hem to the opposite selvage. *Remove pins as you come to them (p. 19).* Stop stitching at the opposite selvage. Backstitch for three or four stitches. Lift the presser foot and *remove the fabric from the machine (p. 19).*

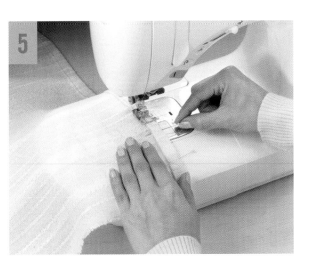

TIP Straight stitching lines are easier to achieve if you watch the presser foot riding over the fold of the fabric and ignore the needle. Sew smoothly at a relaxing pace, with minimal starting and stopping, and without bursts of speed. You have better control of the speed if you operate your foot control with your heel resting on the floor.

6 Repeat steps 2 to 5 for the hem at the opposite end. If your fabric has unsightly selvages, trim them off just inside the tightly woven area, and hem the sides, following steps 2 to 5. Fanfold the entire finished panel into gentle pleats of consistent depth, keeping the right side facing out on the first and last folds. Tie the folded fabric at regular intervals, using ribbon or twill tape (page 27).

7 Drape the folded fabric over the rod, remove the ties, and arrange the folds as shown in the photograph on page 42. Tug gently at the center of the lower folds to shape the swag into a gradual curve.

QUICK REFERENCE

Press under. Place the fabric facedown on your ironing board. Fold the cut edge back; measure and press, keeping the width of the folded edge consistent across the entire edge.

Double-fold hem. Hems for home décor items such as window fashions, pillow sham openings, and shower curtains, are always made with two folds of equal depth, encasing the cut edge in the crease of the outer fold. Pressing the first fold to the total hem depth, in this case 1" (2.5 cm), is more accurate than if you were to fold under 1/2" (1.3 cm) twice.

Self-lined Rectangle VALANCE

Top off a window with this simple, but stylish, self-lined valance. A long rectangle of fabric is folded in half lengthwise, with all the raw edges encased in **SEAMS**. Thus the same fabric forms the face of the valance as well as the **LINING**. The valance is stapled to a mounting board, forming gentle folds at the corners. Plan to mount the board just above the window, extending it 1" (2.5 cm) beyond the window frame on each side. This will allow room to install the board, using an angle iron at each end.

To avoid distracting seams in this valance, select a fabric that can be **RAILROADED**, such as a solid color or a print that can be turned sideways. After trimming the fabric to the necessary width, you can use the excess fabric to cover the mounting board.

WHAT YOU'LL LEARN

How to railroad fabric

How to PIVOT the stitching line at corners

How to encase SEAM ALLOWANCES

How to INTERLINE a treatment

How to install a board-mounted treatment

WHAT YOU'LL NEED

Decorator fabric; see step 1

Drapery lining, if the valance needs to be interlined; see step 1

Thread to match fabric

1 × 4 NOMINAL LUMBER

Heavy-duty stapler; staples

Angle irons and screws, for mounting board

How to Sew a SELF-LINED RECTANGLE VALANCE

1

Width of the window frame:		45"	(115 cm)
Add 1" (2.5 cm) twice	+	1"	(2.5 cm)
	+	1"	(2.5 cm)
to find length of mounting board	=	47"	(120 cm)
Add the desired **FINISHED LENGTH** twice	+	12"	(30.5 cm)
	+	12"	(30.5 cm)
Add 1" (2.5 cm) for seam allowances	+	1"	(2.5 cm)
to find the **CUT LENGTH** of the valance	=	72"	(183 cm)

Purchase the next largest amount of fabric possible.

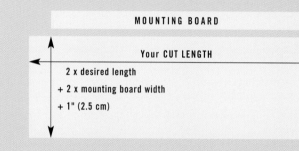

MOUNTING BOARD

Your CUT LENGTH

2 x desired length
+ 2 x mounting board width
+ 1" (2.5 cm)

2

3

4

5

LET'S BEGIN

1 Measure the width of the window frame and determine how high above the frame you want to mount the valance. Then calculate the length of fabric needed for your valance, working with the formula at left. (We used these numbers for our valance on page 46; your numbers will probably be different.)

TIP If you select a print fabric for the valance, fold it in half and hold it up to the window to see if sunlight coming through the fabric will cause the print to show through to the front, muddying the design. If this happens, purchase the same amount of drapery lining, and follow the directions for interlining the valance.

2 Preshrink your fabric (page 33). Cut away the **SELVAGES**, cutting just beyond the tightly woven area. Cut a rectangle of fabric with the length equal to the cut length as determined in step 1. The width is equal to twice the desired valance length plus twice the width of the mounting board plus 1" (2.5 cm) for seam allowances. If you want to interline your valance, cut a rectangle of drapery lining with the same length as the valance fabric; the width is equal to exactly half the width of the valance fabric. Disregard steps 3 and 4 if your valance will not be interlined.

3 Place the interlining over the wrong side of the valance, aligning it to one long edge and the short ends. Pin the layers together near the outer edges, *inserting the pins perpendicular to the edges (p. 19).*

4 Set the stitch length on your machine to sew long stitches. Place the pinned fabric under the presser foot, aligning the cut edges to the ⅜" (1 cm) *seam allowance guide (p. 19)*. Stitch the interlining to the valance fabric along the three pinned sides. From this point on, *handle both layers together as one fabric*.

5 Fold the fabric in half lengthwise, with the right sides together. Align the cut edges at the short ends and along the long side. If your valance is interlined, the long free edge of the interlining should align to the folded edge of the valance. Pin the layers together near the outer raw edges, inserting the pins perpendicular to the edges. On the long side, leave a 10" (25.5 cm) opening.

6 Place the pinned fabric under the presser foot, so that the fold is aligned to the back of the presser foot. Align the cut edges of a short end to the ½" (1.3 cm) seam allowance guide. The bulk of fabric will extend to the left of the machine.

7 *Backstitch (p. 19)* to the fold; stop. Then, stitching forward, stitch the seam, guiding the cut edges along the ½" (1.3 cm) seam allowance guide. *Remove pins as you come to them (p. 19)*.

8 Stop sewing at the first corner, leaving the needle down in the fabric. (Turn the handwheel until the needle is down.) Raise the presser foot and turn the fabric a quarter turn. Lower the presser foot and continue sewing. Stop stitching when you reach the last pin before the opening. Backstitch three or four stitches. *Remove the fabric from the machine (p. 19)*.

CONTINUED

QUICK REFERENCE

Handle both layers together as one fabric.
Fold, stitch, and press both the decorator fabric and the lining fabric together as if they are one fabric, even though the directions may not specifically refer to the interlining.

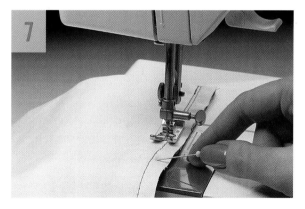

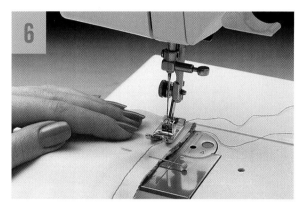

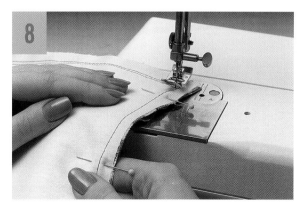

How to Sew a SELF-LINED RECTANGLE VALANCE

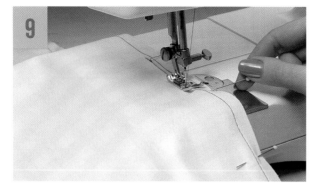

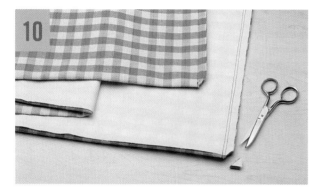

9 Reposition the fabric under the presser foot, just beyond the pin that marks the opposite side of the opening. Backstitch three or four stitches. Then stitch forward, completing the seam on the long edge. Pivot at the opposite corner, and continue stitching to the opposite fold; backstitch three or four stitches. Remove the fabric from the machine. Trim the threads close to the fabric.

10 *Trim the seam allowances diagonally* at the four corners. **PRESS** the seams flat to set the stitches in the fabric. This may seem unnecessary, but it really does give you a better-looking seam in the end.

11 Insert a heavy cardboard tube or a seam roll (page 24) into the opening. Press the seam allowance open, applying light pressure with the tip of the iron down the crease of the seam. Turn back the seam allowances 1/2" (1.3 cm) along the opening, and press.

12 Slip your hand into the opening; grasp one of the far corners of the valance. Pull it through the opening. Repeat this for all of the corners until the entire valance is turned right side out. Insert a point turner or similar tool into the valance through the opening, gently pushing the points out to form *perfect corners.*

13 Press the entire valance, including the fold at the lower edge. Pin the opening closed. Place the valance under the presser foot just behind the opening; the needle should be aligned to sew just inside the folded edges. Stitch the opening closed, backstitching a few stitches at the beginning and end of the stitching line. Remember to remove pins as you come to them.

14 Cut the mounting board 2" (5 cm) longer than the measured width of the window frame; cover it with fabric, if desired. Attach angle irons to the underside near the ends, with the corners aligned to the board back. Mount the board to the wall just above and outside the frame. Remove the board, leaving the angle irons on the wall. Center the valance over the top of the mounting board with the long stitched edge along the back of the board. The valance should extend the same distance off both ends and off the front of the board.

QUICK REFERENCE

Trim the seam allowances diagonally. This step eliminates the excess bulk at the corners, allowing them to lie flat and square after turning the valance right side out.

Perfect corners. The corners of your valance should be sharply squared, not rounded. To improve the appearance of a slightly rounded corner, you can push a pointed utensil into the corner from inside the valance to force the stitches out to the corner. An inexpensive specialty tool, called a point turner, works well; or you can use a large knitting needle, a ballpoint pen with the inkball retracted, or something similar. Use light pressure, though, so that you don't punch a hole in the corner.

15 Staple the valance to the mounting board, inserting the staples near the back of the board. Begin in the center and work toward the ends, spacing the staples 4" to 6" (10 to 15 cm) apart. Mount the valance on the angle irons, replacing the screws in their original holes. Adjust the front corners of the valance to fall in gently rounded folds as shown on page 46.

Strap-tied VALANCE

The versatile style of this **LINED-TO-THE-EDGE** board-mounted valance makes it suitable for many decorating schemes. Fabric choice determines whether it has a sleek, contemporary look; cozy, country appeal; or classic, traditional elegance. Excess length, fanfolded at the lower edge, is held in place with straps, forming pleated wings at the corners and a gentle swag in the middle.

Using one 54" (137 cm) width of decorator fabric, this valance is suitable for windows with inside frame measurements of 53" (134.5 cm) or less, with a frame depth deep enough to accommodate the mounting board.

WHAT YOU'LL LEARN

How to line a window treatment

How to reduce bulk at square corners

How to stitch and turn long straps

WHAT YOU'LL NEED

Two decorator fabrics; one for the valance and one for the **LINING** and straps

Thread to match

3/4" (2 cm) wooden dowel

Mounting board; 1 x 2 NOMINAL LUMBER

Heavy-duty stapler; staples

How to Sew a STRAP-TIED VALANCE

1

Desired FINISHED LENGTH at the strap:		12"	(30.5 cm)
Add 24" (61 cm) for fanfolds	+	24"	(61 cm)
Add 1/2" (1.3 cm) for seam allowance	+	1/2"	(1.3 cm)
Add the mounting board width	+	1 1/2"	(3.8 cm)
to find the CUT LENGTH of the valance	=	38"	(96.5 cm)

Add 1/2 yd. (0.5 m) of fabric to allow for covering the mounting board and making the straps. Purchase the next largest amount possible for each of the two fabrics.

1 Determine how long you want your valance, measured at the strap. The center will swag down a distance equal to about one-sixth the width of the valance. Then calculate the length of fabric needed for your valance, working with the formula at left. (We used these numbers for our valance on page 52; your numbers will probably be different.)

TIP If you select two print fabrics for the valance, layer them and hold them up to the window to see if sunlight coming through the fabric will cause the lining print to show through to the front, muddying the design. If this happens, purchase the same amount of drapery lining, and follow the directions for INTERLINING the valance.

2 Preshrink your fabric (page 33). Cut away the SELVAGES, cutting just beyond the tightly woven area. Cut a rectangle of fabric with the length equal to the cut length as determined in step 1. The CUT WIDTH is equal to the inside frame measurement of the window plus 1" (2.5 cm) for SEAM ALLOWANCES. Cut the lining fabric to the same size. If you want to interline your valance, cut drapery lining to the same size as the valance and lining pieces. Disregard steps 3 and 4 if your valance will not be interlined.

3 Place the interlining over the wrong side of the valance, aligning all the cut edges. Pin the layers together near the outer edges, *inserting the pins perpendicular to the edge (p. 19).*

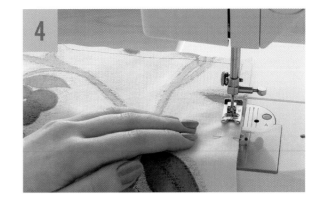

4 Place the pinned fabric under the presser foot, aligning the cut edges to the 3/8" (1 cm) *seam allowance guide (p. 19). Machine-baste* the interlining to the valance fabric along the pinned sides. From this point on, *handle both layers together as one fabric (p. 49).*

TIP Most machines have a handy thread cutter located within a few inches (centimeters) of the presser foot. By using this thread cutter, you are also pulling enough thread through the needle and up from the bobbin to help you prevent a THREAD JAM at the start of your next seam.

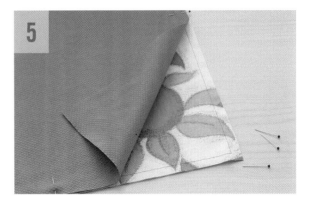

5 Place the lining over the valance fabric, right sides together. Pin the fabrics together along the sides and lower edge, inserting the pins perpendicular to the edge.

6 Place the pinned fabric under the presser foot, with the upper edge aligned to the back of the presser foot and the cut edges to the 1/2" (1.3 cm) seam allowance guide on the bed of your machine. The bulk of the fabric will extend to the left of the machine. *Backstitch (p. 19)* a few stitches. Then, stitching forward, stitch the **SEAM**, guiding the cut edges along the 1/2" (1.3 cm) seam allowance guide. *Remove pins as you come to them (p. 19).*

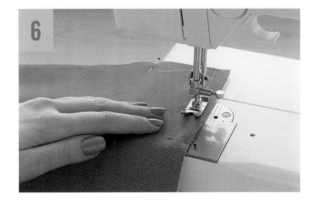

QUICK REFERENCE

Machine-baste. Set the stitch length on your machine to sew long stitches. This is done to hold the two fabrics together until they are secured in a seam. Because the stitches are long, the fabric may want to pucker. To avoid this, hold the fabric taut, with one hand in front of the presser foot and the other hand behind it.

CONTINUED

How to Sew a STRAP-TIED VALANCE

7 Stop stitching 1/2" (1.3 cm) from the first corner, leaving the needle down in the fabric. (Turn the handwheel until the needle is down.) Raise the presser foot and turn the fabric a quarter turn. Lower the presser foot and continue stitching, **PIVOTING** in this manner at the other corner. Stitch the opposite side, backstitching a few stitches at the upper edge. *Remove the fabric from the machine (p. 19).*

8 *Trim the seam allowances diagonally (p. 51)* at the two corners. **PRESS** the seams flat to set the stitching line in the fabric. Insert a seam roll or heavy cardboard tube into the open end, and press the seam allowances open.

9 Turn the valance right side out. Insert a point turner or other tool into the valance through the opening to form *perfect corners (p. 51)*. Press the entire valance. Pin the upper edges together. Stitch 3/8" (1 cm) from the edges.

10 Cut two strips of fabric, 4" (10 cm) wide, from the **CROSSWISE GRAIN**, for the straps. The cut length of the straps is equal to twice the desired finished length plus 4" (10 cm). Fold one strap in half lengthwise, with the right sides together. Pin the layers together along the long raw edges. Stitch a 1/2" (1.3 cm) seam down the long side, backstitching a few stitches at the beginning and end of the seam.

11 Press the seam flat, keeping the iron away from the folded edge. Insert a 3/4" (2 cm) wood dowel into the tube, centering it under the seam. Press the seam allowances open over the dowel. The dowel helps you press only the seam without pressing unwanted creases into the rest of the strap.

12 Tie a safety pin to a string, cut longer than the strap. Insert the safety pin into one end of the strap, allowing the weight of the pin to pull the string through the strap. Then secure the pin to the inside of the strap at the opposite end.

13 Pull on the string to turn the strap right side out, gently working the fabric over the safety pin. Remove the pin.

CONTINUED

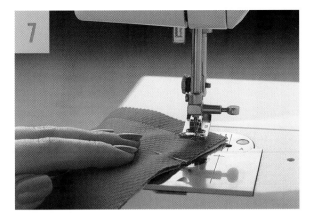

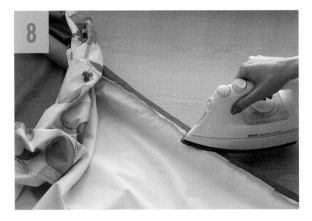

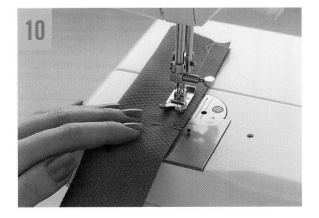

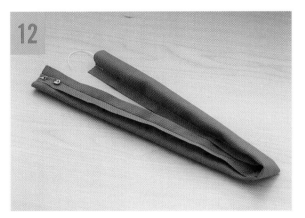

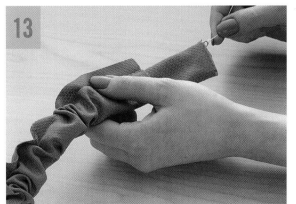

How to Sew a STRAP-TIED VALANCE

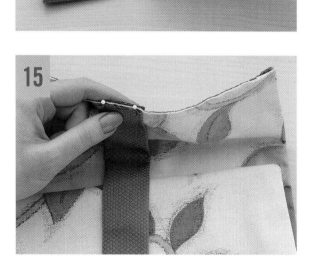

14 Press the strap flat, centering the seam on the back of the strap.

15 Pin the straps, right side up, to the upper edge of the valance, placing them a distance from the sides equal to about one-sixth the total width of the valance. Wrap the straps under the valance, and pin the opposite ends in place. Stitch the straps in place, 3/8" (1 cm) from the edges.

16 *Finish the raw edges* together across the top of the valance, using a **ZIGZAG** stitch set at medium width and medium length. Stitch so the right swing of the needle just clears the fabric edge.

17 Cut the mounting board 1/2" (1.3 cm) shorter than the inside width of the window frame; cover it with fabric, if desired. Holding the board against the top inside of the window frame, flush with the frame front, predrill mounting holes through the board and into the frame. Center the valance over the top of the mounting board, with the finished edge along the back of the board.

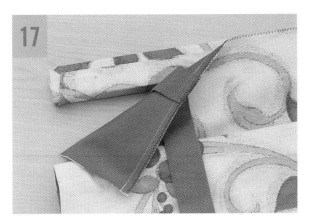

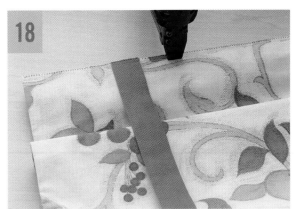

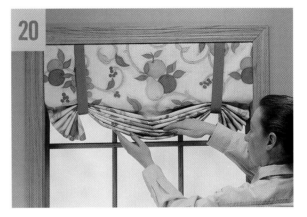

18 Staple the valance to the mounting board, inserting the staples near the back of the board. Begin in the center and work toward the ends, spacing the staples 4" to 6" (10 to 15 cm) apart. Apply two staples at each strap.

19 Mount the valance inside the window frame, inserting screws through the predrilled holes. Fanfold the lower 24" (61 cm) of the valance into five or six even pleats, beginning by folding under the lower edge toward the lining. Slip the pleats into the straps.

20 Pull the pleats into a gentle swag at the center. Adjust the folds as necessary near the straps.

QUICK REFERENCE

Finish the raw edges. Abrasion and laundering will cause yarns to ravel off the raw edges of any woven fabric unless you do something to prevent it. Zigzag stitches sewn over the edge lock the outer yarns in place. This is a suitable way to finish edges that normally don't show.

MORE IDEAS

Make three lightweight to sheer valances in lengths that vary by 2" (5 cm). Stack and mount them for a delicate layered look.

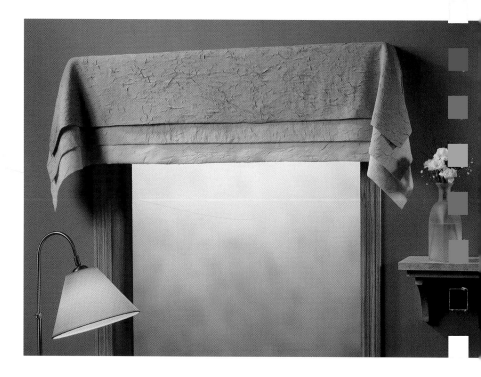

Convert this style into a coach valance. Reduce the excess length to 12" (30.5 cm) instead of 24" (61 cm). Roll the lower edge around a 1" (2.5 cm) wooden dowel, rolling from the right side, to expose the lining. Apply double-stick tape inside the straps, if necessary, to keep the fabric from unrolling. Paint the dowel ends to match the lining. Make four straps instead of two. Cut the straps 30" (76 cm) long, and stitch across one end before turning them right side out. Or use four lengths of sturdy ribbon. Tie them in bows or simple knots at the bottom of the valance.

Sew tent flap curtains, following steps 2 to 9 and 16 to 19; disregard the references to the straps and fanfolding. Determine the cut length of the fabric, lining, and interlining by adding 1/2" (1.3 cm) seam allowance and the width of the mounting board to the desired finished length of the curtain. For example: 45" + 1/2" + 1 1/2" = 47" (115 cm + 1.3 cm + 3.8 cm = 120 cm) Hand-stitch a decorative ring to one corner of the curtain. Pull back the curtain, and hook the ring on a decorative hook installed on the window frame or wall.

Knot two chair ties together to form a cord-and-tassel swag. Attach it to the valance as shown, using hand stitches.

Window TOPPER

This easy stylish window topper has lots of creative possibilities. Designed as a decorative accent over a shade or blinds, it is simply a flat **LINED-TO-THE-EDGE** shape that flips over a decorative rod. Buttonholes and buttons secure the topper and add splashes of color. A layer of lining fabric between the front and back fabrics, called **INTERLINING**, adds body and support for the buttonholes. Because you first create a paper pattern, you can design the topper with straight, curved, or pointed lower edges. Select firmly woven fabrics in two coordinating colors or a **NONDIRECTIONAL PRINT** and a solid color, one for the front and one for the back.

WHAT YOU'LL LEARN

If you can measure, draw lines, and cut paper, you can design a window topper!

How to sew buttonholes and buttons

How to shape perfect points and corners

WHAT YOU'LL NEED

Decorative curtain rod

Two coordinating firmly woven fabrics, amount determined after making pattern

Drapery lining fabric, amount determined after making pattern

Wide craft paper

Quilting ruler or carpenter's square

Thread to blend with the fabrics

Paper-backed fusible web

Buttons in desired sizes and colors

Liquid fray preventer

Buttonhole cutter

How to Sew a WINDOW TOPPER

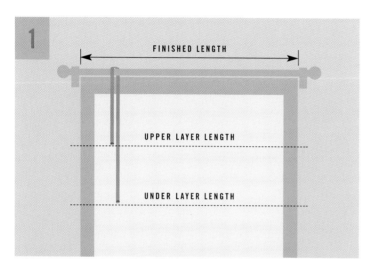

1

FINISHED LENGTH

UPPER LAYER LENGTH

UNDER LAYER LENGTH

2

- -

LET'S BEGIN

- -

1 Mount the rod so that the top is even with the top of the window frame or slightly higher. The brackets should be just outside the frame or at least 1" (2.5 cm) beyond any existing treatment. Measure from bracket to bracket to determine the width of the topper pattern. Hang a tape measure over the rod to determine the length of the pattern.

TIP The topper should be at least long enough to cover a raised blind or shade. For a pleasing proportion, it should cover no more than one-third of the window.

2 Cut a paper pattern to these dimensions, using a quilting ruler or carpenter's square for accuracy. Shape the lower edges into one or more shallow curves or points, if you desire, and hang it over the rod. Stand back for a look, and make any final adjustments. Draw a line where the pattern crosses the rod. Measure the pattern and buy equal amounts of both fabrics and the interlining. Preshrink (page 33) all three fabrics if you intend to launder the topper.

TIP If the window is narrower than the fabric, purchase slightly more fabric than the pattern length. You will align the pattern vertically to the LENGTHWISE GRAIN of the fabric. If the window is wider than the fabric, purchase slightly more fabric than the pattern width. You will align the pattern vertically to the CROSSWISE GRAIN.

3 Pin the pattern over one of the fabrics. The outer edge of the pattern is the stitching line for the topper. Mark the cutting line on the fabric, 1/2" (1.3 cm) beyond the pattern edge. Cut out the fabric. Remove the pattern.

4 Place the other fabric faceup over the interlining. Pin the cut fabric facedown over both layers, aligning all grainlines. *Insert the pins* near and *perpendicular to the cut edges (p. 19).* Cut the other layers. *Leave the pins in the fabric.*

CONTINUED

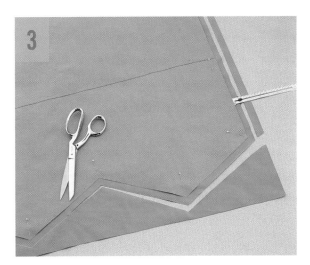

How to Sew a WINDOW TOPPER

CONTINUED

----

5 Set the machine for a straight stitch of 12 stitches per inch, which equals 2 mm. Place the fabric under the presser foot near the center of one long edge, so that the cut edges are aligned to the 1/2" (1.3 cm) *seam allowance guide (p. 19). Backstitch (p. 19)* a few stitches. Then stitch forward, guiding the cut edges along the 1/2" (1.3 cm) seam allowance guide. *Remove pins as you come to them (p. 19).*

6 Stop stitching at the first corner, leaving the needle down in the fabric. (Turn the handwheel until the needle is down.) Raise the presser foot, and turn the fabric. Lower the presser foot, and continue stitching. **PIVOT** in the same way at each corner.

7 Stop stitching about 10" (25.5 cm) from where you began; backstitch, leaving an opening for turning the topper right side out. *Remove the fabric from the machine (p. 19). Trim the seam allowances diagonally at outer corners (p. 51). Clip to, but not through,* the stitches at any inner corners.

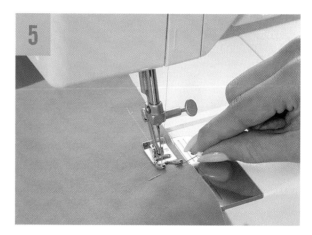

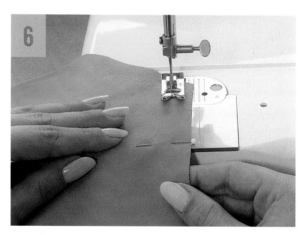

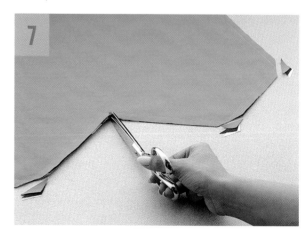

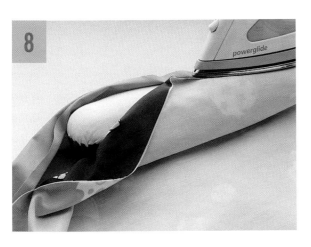

QUICK REFERENCE

Clip to, but not through. This will allow the fabric to lay smoothly without puckering when the topper is turned right side out. Be careful not to cut the stitches, or a hole will develop in the seam.

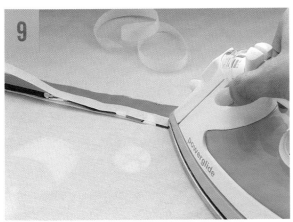

8 **PRESS** the seams flat to set the stitching line in the fabric. Insert a heavy cardboard tube or a seam roll (page 24) into the opening. Press the seam allowances open, applying light pressure with the tip of the iron down the crease of the seam.

9 Turn back the seam allowances 1/2" (1.3 cm) along the opening, and press. (On one side you will also be turning back the interlining.) Cut a 10" (25.5 cm) strip of 3/8" (1 cm) paper-backed fusible web (page 26). Place the strip over the seam allowance at the opening, just inside the folded edge. Press over the strip to fuse it to the seam allowance, following the manufacturer's directions.

CONTINUED

How to Sew a WINDOW TOPPER

CONTINUED

----

10 Turn the valance right side out through the opening. Insert a point turner or similar tool into the opening and gently push any pivot points out to form *perfect corners (p. 51)*. Push the seam out so that it is centered all around the outer edge. Press the entire valance. Remove the protective paper backing from the fusible web at the opening. Align the folded edges of the opening. Press over the opening to fuse it closed.

11 Place the topper on a flat surface. Using the marked line on the pattern as a guide, fold the upper flap down. Plan and mark the placement for vertical buttonholes, keeping the lower ends of the buttonholes at least 1" (2.5 cm) above the lower edge of the flap. Mark lines that equal the diameter plus the thickness of the buttons.

If you prefer, you can opt not to make buttonholes, and simply sew the buttons onto the topper through both layers. Then slip the rod through the topper to mount it. However, this is a good opportunity to learn how to make buttonholes. Practice on a triple layer of scrap fabric until you are sure of the technique and the buttonhole length.

12 Attach your buttonhole presser foot or buttonhole attachment. Follow the instructions in your owner's manual to stitch the buttonholes over the marked lines. Apply liquid fray preventer (page 25) to the buttonholes; allow it to dry. Cut the buttonholes open, using a buttonhole cutter or small, sharp scissors.

13 Refold the topper. Mark the placements for the buttons on the lower layer, inserting the marker through the bottom of each buttonhole. Sew the buttons to the topper, as on page 39. Hang the window topper over the rod.

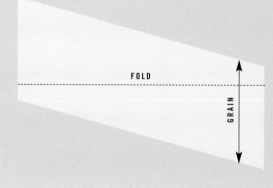

MORE IDEAS

Dragonflies dart about in this cheerful
cotton print. Large buttons covered in the
striped fabric line up under the rod. The
pattern for this topper (diagram) is actually
a parallelogram. The sides are aligned
to the grain of the fabric; the angled lower
edges are sewn on the BIAS.

FOLD

GRAIN

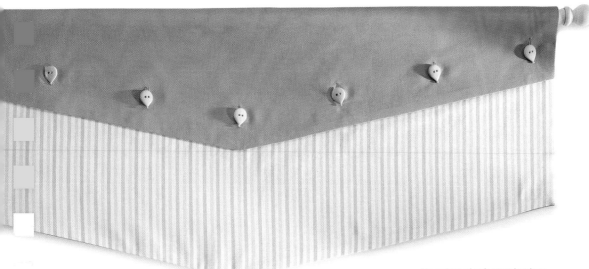

The colors of soft pastel stripes are repeated with fancy balloon buttons positioned along the angled lower edges. Sew buttonholes along the grainline, even though the edge runs on the bias.

Curved seam allowances are trimmed to 1/4" (6 mm) for ease in turning right side out. Ribbon ties are cut 18" (46 cm) long and stitched to the under layer instead of buttons. The ribbon ends are then pulled through small buttonholes and tied into bows, anchoring the topper over the pole.

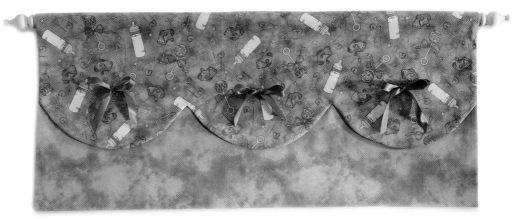

Relaxed Rod-pocket CURTAINS

Many window fashions are hung from a pole or rod by means of a "pocket" or **CASING** sewn along the upper edge. These contemporary curtains are designed with deep, loose rod pockets. They look great hanging from narrow metal rods with decorative finials. Because rod-pocket styles are intended to be stationary, they can be designed as two separate panels hung at the sides of a window or as two panels that touch at the top center and are parted and pulled back to the sides. One continuous panel may cover the window or be pulled to one side or even tied in the center. For a luxurious look, the curtains can be made with extra length so that the hem brushes or puddles on the floor.

WHAT YOU'LL LEARN

How fullness affects the look of the curtain, and how to use fullness in calculating the amount of fabric to buy

How to match the design in a decorator print

How to make a rod pocket or casing

How to make deep double-fold hems

Where to put drapery weights and how to attach them

WHAT YOU'LL NEED

Decorator fabric, amount determined by working through the chart in step 1

Thread to match the fabric

Drapery weights, one for each lower corner and one for each vertical seam

Curtain rod and mounting hardware

How to Sew a RELAXED ROD-POCKET CURTAIN

1

FINISHED LENGTH, measured from the top of the rod to the bottom of the treatment:	84"	(213.5 cm)
Add 8" (20.5 cm) for the total hem depth	+ 8"	(20.5 cm)
Add 5½" (14 cm) for the rod pocket depth	+ 5½"	(14 cm)
Add ½" (1.3 cm) for ease	+ ½"	(1.3 cm)
to find the **CUT LENGTH** of each piece (see note below)	= 98"	(249 cm)
Multiply the total desired width of coverage	45"	(115 cm)
by the desired **FULLNESS**	× 2	
to find the total finished width	= 90"	(229 cm)
Add 3" (7.5 cm) for each side hem depth	+ 3"	(7.5 cm)
	+ 3"	(7.5 cm)
	+ 3"	(7.5 cm)
	+ 3"	(7.5 cm)
To find the total **CUT WIDTH** needed	= 102"	(259 cm)
Divide the total cut width by the fabric width	÷ 54"	(137 cm)
Round the number up to the nearest whole number	= 1.9	
to find the number of fabric widths needed	2	
Multiply this number by the cut length	× 98"	(249 cm)
to find the length to buy	= 196"	(498 cm)

If you buy a fabric with a **PATTERN REPEAT,** follow the chart until you have determined the cut length. Your actual cut length must be rounded up to the next number evenly divisible by the pattern repeat. For instance, if the pattern repeat is 15" (38 cm), your cut length will be 105" (267 cm), not 98" (249 cm), because 105" (266) can be evenly divided by 15 (38). Proceed with the chart using this revised cut length measurement. Because fabric stores sell fabric in whole yards (meters) or eighths of a yard (fractions of a meter), purchase the next largest amount.

LET'S BEGIN

1 Install the rod just above the window frame, following the manufacturer's directions. Measure the window and calculate the length of fabric needed for your curtain, working with the formula at left. (We used these numbers for our curtain on page 72; your numbers will probably be different.)

 TIP A single width of 54" (137 cm) decorator fabric, hemmed and gathered onto a rod at one-and-one-half times fullness, will cover 32" (81.5 cm). The same panel gathered onto the rod at two times fullness will cover 24" (61 cm). Use less fullness for heavier fabrics or to allow a large pattern to be more apparent. Use more fullness for lighter-weight fabrics to create more body.

2 Preshrink your fabric (page 33). Measure and mark the location of each cut along the selvage. Cut the pieces, following the cutting guidelines on page 34. If your fabric has a pattern to match, follow the steps on page 36 to join fabric widths, and then jump to step 4, opposite. If you do not have to match a pattern, cut away the selvages, cutting just beyond the tightly woven area.

3 Pin two pieces together along the vertical edges, *inserting the pins perpendicular to the edges (p. 19).* Stitch ½" (1.3 cm) **SEAM**, *backstitching (p. 19)* a few stitches at the beginning and end of the seam. *Remove the pins as you come to them (p. 19).* Repeat this step until you have sewn all the pieces together for each curtain panel. If there are any *half widths,* sew them onto outer sides of panels.

4 For each seam, *finish the raw edges (p. 59)* together, using a **ZIGZAG STITCH** set at medium width and medium length. Stitch so the right-hand swing of the needle just clears the fabric edges. **PRESS** all of the seam allowances *to one side.*

5 Place the curtain facedown on an ironing surface. *Press under (p. 45)* lower edge 8" (20.5 cm), for hem. Unfold the pressed edge. Turn the cut edge back, aligning it to the pressed foldline; press outer fold.

QUICK REFERENCE

Round up to the nearest whole number. Most window treatments that have some amount of fullness in them, including rod-pocket treatments, are sewn using full and half widths of fabric. Even if your treatment requires two and one-half widths of fabric, you have to purchase three full widths, and your yardage requirements have to be determined by rounding up to the nearest whole number.

Half widths are always added at the outer edge of a curtain or valance panel. The seam is sewn along the edge that had the selvage; the side hem is sewn along the edge that was the center of the fabric width. (This is the only way you are able to match the pattern, if there is one.)

To one side. If there are two curtain panels, the seams of each panel are pressed away from the center.

CONTINUED

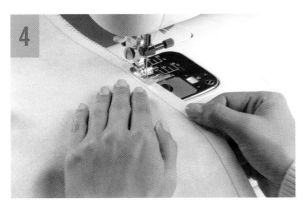

How to Sew a RELAXED ROD-POCKET CURTAIN

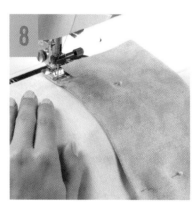

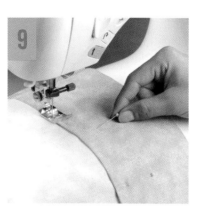

CONTINUED

----

6 Thread a hand needle with a double strand of thread (page 38). Place a drapery weight over the seam allowances, aligning the bottom of the weight to the bottom of the curtain. Hand-tack the upper flap of the weight to the seam allowances. Repeat at the bottom of all the seams.

7 Refold the hem along the pressed foldlines, encasing the raw edge to form a 4" (10 cm) *double-fold hem (p. 45).* Pin the hem, inserting the pins perpendicular to the foldlines.

8 Place the hem under the presser foot of the machine, with the wrong side of the curtain facing up. The bulk of the fabric is positioned to the left of the machine. The side edge is under the presser foot, with the needle aligned to enter the fabric just inside the inner fold.

9 Stitch the hem along the inner fold, backstitching a few stitches at the beginning and end. Remove pins as you come to them.

TIP Double-fold bottom hems on floor-length curtains and curtains that brush on the floor measure a total of 8" (20.5 cm): 4" (10 cm) turned under twice. Double-fold hems on curtains that puddle on the floor measure a total of 2" (5 cm): 1" (2.5 cm) turned under twice. Double-fold side hems on curtains measure a total of 3" (7.5 cm): 1½" (3.8 cm) turned under twice. Double-fold bottom hems on valances measure a total of 4" (10 cm): 2" (5 cm) turned under twice.

10 Repeat steps 5 to 9 for the side hems, pressing under 3" (7.5 cm) first, instead of 8" (20.5 cm). Before refolding the side hems, slip a drapery weight into the space between the layers of the lower hem. It will be locked in place when you stitch.

TIP You may have difficulty sewing past the weight because of its thickness. Just as the presser foot toes reach the weight, stop with your needle down in the fabric and raise the presser foot. Slip another weight under the foot on the opposite side so the foot can ride on an even surface. Stitch slowly past the weight. Then stop with the needle down in the fabric, remove the loose weight, and continue on.

11 Press under ½" (1.3 cm) along the upper edge. Then, measuring from the pressed fold-line, press under 5" (12.7 cm) for the rod pocket. Insert pins along the lower foldline.

12 Place the folded upper edge under the presser foot of the machine, with the wrong side of the curtain facing up. The bulk of the fabric is positioned to the left of the machine. The side hem should be under the presser foot, with the needle aligned to enter the fabric along the lower fold.

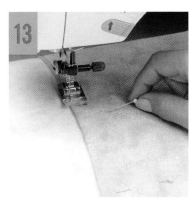

13 Stitch along the lower fold, across the entire width; backstitch a few stitches at the beginning and the end. Remove pins as you come to them. This stitching line is the bottom of the rod pocket.

14 Press the curtain one more time. Insert the rod into the rod pocket. Mount the rod on the brackets, following the instructions that came with the rod. Distribute the fullness evenly along the rod, taking up the desired finished width.

TIP Tape a small plastic bag over the end of the rod to make it slide more easily into the rod pocket.

PLACEMATS and NAPKINS

S park up your dining room table or breakfast nook with reversible octagonal placemats. These placemats are **LINED TO THE EDGE** and can be made reversible by selecting two decorator fabrics. Welting (page 27), sewn into the outer edge of the placemat, is available in different sizes and colors. For ease of application, choose welting no larger than 3/16" (4.5 mm). Make napkins to match, simply by cutting, pressing, and hemming. If you want to be able to launder the placemats and napkins, choose fabrics that are washable and be sure to preshrink (page 33) the fabrics and the welting before you start cutting.

WHAT YOU'LL LEARN

How to cut fabric using a paper pattern

How to insert narrow welting into a seam

How to make neat corners and points

How to stitch a mitered double-fold hem

WHAT YOU'LL NEED

For four sets:

Craft paper for drawing a pattern

3/4 yd. (0.7 m) fabric for placemat fronts

3/4 yd. (0.7 m) fabric for placemat backs

7 yd. (6.4 m) welting

1 yd. (0.92 m) fabric for napkins

Thread to match fabrics

How to Sew a PLACEMAT

1 Draw a 13" × 19" (33 × 48.5 cm) rectangle on craft paper. Mark a point 3½" (9 cm) from each corner. Draw diagonal lines across each corner connecting marks; cut off the corners.

2 Preshrink the fabrics (page 33). To preshrink the welting, wrap it into large loops and tie it in the middle with a large loose knot. Soak the welting in warm water; squeeze out excess moisture. Place it in a net laundry bag or nylon stocking before tossing it in the dryer. This will keep it from getting too tangled.

3 Fold the fabric for the placemat front in half lengthwise, aligning the **SELVAGES**. Place the paper pattern with one short edge running parallel to and just beyond the selvages. This will ensure that the placemat is cut on-grain. Pin the pattern in place through both layers of fabric inserting pins about every 3" (7.5 cm) around the outer edge. Cut out the placemat. Remove the pins and cut two more fronts, following the same procedure. Then cut four placemat backs from the other fabric.

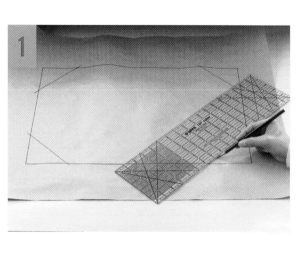

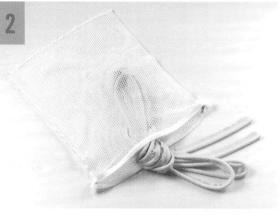

4 **PRESS** the flat edge of the welt-ing if necessary. Pin the welting to the right side of the placemat front along the outer edge, keeping the raw edges aligned and the welting relaxed. Plan for the ends to overlap along one long edge and leave tails unpinned. *Insert the pins perpendicular to the edges (p. 19).*

TIP Keep the welting relaxed as you pin and actually "crowd" the welting slightly at the corners so that it will lie flat when it is turned to its final position.

5 Clip into the seam allowance of the welting at each corner of the placemat at the exact point where the welting must bend. *Clip to, but not through (p. 67)* the stitching line, so that the welting seam allowances spread open and lie flat. Pin securely, keeping the raw edges of the welting and placemat aligned.

6 Set the machine for a straight stitch of 10 stitches per inch, which equals 2.5 mm. Attach the zipper foot (page 11) and adjust it to the right of the needle. If your foot is not adjustable, adjust the needle to the left of the foot. Place the fabric under the presser foot 2" (5 cm) from the end of the welting. Slowly stitch the welting to the fabric, stitching over the existing stitches in the welting. *Remove pins as you come to them (p. 19).*

CONTINUED

How to Sew a PLACEMAT

- -

CONTINUED

- -

7 When you reach a corner, stop with the needle down in the fabric at the point of the clip. Lift the presser foot and **PIVOT** the fabric so the stitching line of the welting on the next side is in line with the needle. Lower the presser foot and continue stitching around the placemat, pivoting at each corner.

8 Stop stitching 2" (5 cm) from the point where the ends of the welting will meet. Cut off the end of the welting so it overlaps the beginning end by 1" (2.5 cm). Remove the stitching from the overlapping end of the welting, exposing the inner cording; trim the end of the cording so it just meets the other end.

9 Fold under 1/2" (1.3 cm) of the fabric on the overlapping end of the welting. Wrap it around the beginning and finish stitching it to the placemat, overlapping the stitches 1/2" (1.3 cm) where they meet.

10 Press along the stitching line with the tip of your iron to relax the fabric and set the seam. Check that the fabric does not ripple or draw up where you have attached the welting.

11 Pin the placemat front over the back, right sides together, encasing the welting between the layers and aligning the outer edges. Leave a 7" (18 cm) opening unpinned along one side. Place the placemat under the presser foot, back side down, just ahead of the unpinned area. Remove the pin marking the end of the opening before lowering the presser foot.

12 *Backstitch (p. 19)* three or four stitches; then stitch forward *over the previous stitches,* actually "crowding" the welting with the zipper foot as you stitch. Pivot at each corner, and stop stitching at the opposite side of the opening. Backstitch three or four stitches, and *remove the fabric from the machine (p. 19).*

CONTINUED

QUICK REFERENCE

Over the previous stitches. The second stitching line must be exactly over the first stitching line or slightly closer to the welting, so that the first stitching line does not show after the placemat is turned right side out.

How to Sew a PLACEMAT

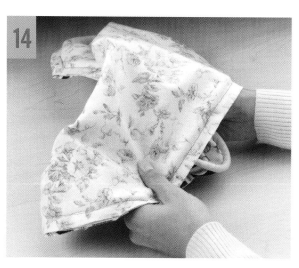

CONTINUED

----

13 *Trim the seam allowances diagonally (p. 51)* at each corner. Turn back and press the back seam allowance 1/2" (1.3 cm) from the edge in the unstitched area.

14 Reach in through the unstitched opening to grasp the opposite side of the placemat and pull it through the opening. Turn the placemat right side out.

15 Use a point turner to push out the corners, if necessary. Press the placemat up to the welting as you smooth and tug the welting out to the edge with your fingers. Slipstitch the opening closed, following the directions on page 38.

How to Sew NAPKINS

1 Cut squares for the napkins 1" (2.5 cm) larger than the desired finished size. Press under ½" (1.3 cm) on each side of the napkin. Unfold the corner, and refold it diagonally so that the pressed folds match. Press the diagonal fold, and trim the corner as shown. Repeat for each corner.

TIP For the most efficient use of your fabric, cut three 15" (38 cm) squares from 45" (115 cm) fabric or 18" (46 cm) squares from 54" (137 cm) fabric.

2 Fold the raw edges under to meet the pressed fold, forming a ¼" (6 mm) *double-fold hem (p. 45)*. The corners will form neat diagonal folds. Press the folds; pin only if necessary.

3 Stitch the hem close to the inner fold, using a short straight stitch and beginning along one side. At the corners, stop with the needle down in the fabric, between the diagonal folds, and pivot. Overlap the stitches about ½" (1.3 cm) where they meet.

Banded TABLECLOTH

Add a dash of decorating spice to your dining area with a custom banded tablecloth. A pleasing **DROP LENGTH** for dining tables is about 10" (25.5 cm). Decorator fabrics that are 54" (137 cm) wide are often not wide enough, especially after they have been hemmed. In this version, a 4" (10 cm) band of contrasting fabric is added around the lower edge, giving the tablecloth extra length and a designer touch. The **MITERED** corners of the band give it a professional look and are easier to sew than you might think. Careful measuring and cutting are the key ingredients to a perfect tablecloth.

WHAT YOU'LL LEARN

How to measure, mark, and cut with precision

How to finish an edge with a band

How to miter a corner

How to use a disappearing fabric marker

WHAT YOU'LL NEED

Fabric for the tablecloth center, 54" or 60" (137 or 152.5 cm) wide; 1 yd. (0.92 m) longer than the tabletop length

Contrasting fabric for the band, 1⅓ yd. (1.23 m) longer than the tabletop length

Thread to match the band fabric

Disappearing marker (air or water soluble)

How to Sew a BANDED TABLECLOTH

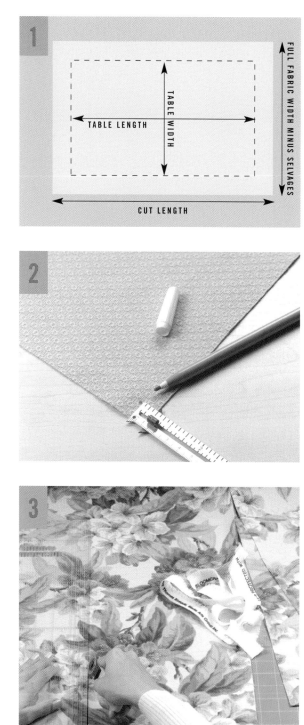

1 Preshrink the fabrics (page 33). Cut off the **SELVAGES** evenly, just beyond the tightly woven area. *Square off one end of the fabric,* following the cutting directions on page 34. Measure your tabletop width and subtract the measurement from the fabric width. Record the difference. Measure and mark the fabric length equal to the tabletop length plus the width difference you recorded. Cut the fabric squarely at the mark.

2 Mark a dot ¹/₂" (1.3 cm) from each corner on the center panel, using a fabric marker with disappearing ink (page 22). Measure the distance between dots on one long side and one short side. Record the measurements.

3 Cut the selvages from the band fabric. Cut the band fabric into four 9" (23 cm) strips running parallel to the **LENGTHWISE GRAIN.**

QUICK REFERENCE

Square off one end of the fabric. In order for the tablecloth to fit the table correctly and for the band to be sewn with accuracy, the fabric must be cut with perfect 90-degree corners.

4 Fold one end of one band strip in half lengthwise. Cut the end at a perfect 45-degree angle starting at the end of the fold. Unfold the strip. Mark short intersecting lines at the 45-degree corners on the 1/2" (1.3 cm) seamlines. Mark a dot 1/2" (1.3 cm) from the corner on the square point.

TIP If you don't have a ruler of other device with markings for cutting the 45-degree angle, fold a large square of paper in half diagonally, and use that as a pattern.

5 Place a pin on the opposite end of the strip a distance from the intersecting lines equal to the distance between dots on one long side of the center panel. Using the angled end as a guide and aligning the intersecting lines to the pin, angle-cut the other end. Cut a band for the other long side to match. Mark intersecting lines as in step 4.

CONTINUED

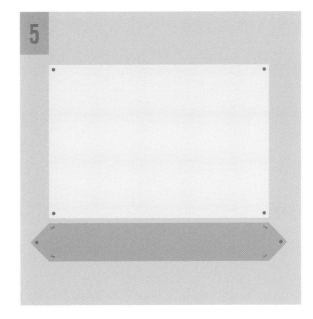

How to Sew a BANDED TABLECLOTH

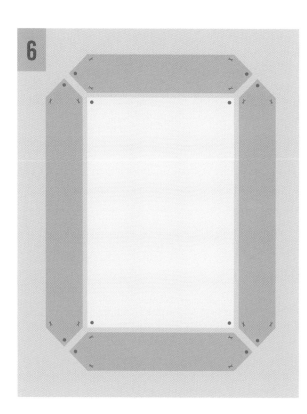

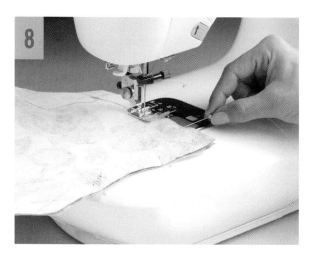

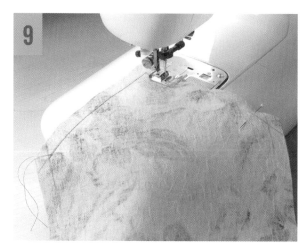

CONTINUED

6 Repeat steps 4 and 5 for the short bands, making the distance between intersecting lines equal to the distance between dots on the short sides of the center panel.

7 Pin the angled end of a short band to the angled end of a long band, right sides together, matching the dots and raw edges. *Insert the pins perpendicular to the edges (p. 19).*

8 Place the fabric under the presser foot so the angled edges align to the 1/2" (1.3 cm) *seam allowance guide (p. 19)* and the needle will enter the fabric just ahead of the intersection. *Backstitch (p. 19)* to the intersection. Then stitch forward guiding the raw edges along the 1/2" (1.3 cm) seam guide. *Remove pins as you come to them (p. 19).*

9 Stop with the needle down in the fabric at the marked dot on the square corner. Raise the presser foot; **PIVOT** the fabric. Lower the presser foot and continue stitching to the other marked intersection. Backstitch a few stitches. *Remove the fabric from the machine (p. 19).*

10 Repeat steps 7 to 9 to join the remaining ends of the band strips, alternating long and short, until you have sewn all of them into a large circle. Trim the seam allowances to 1/4" (6 mm). At the square corners, *trim the seam allowances diagonally (p. 51)* close to the pivot point. **PRESS** the seam allowances open.

11 *Press under (p. 45)* 1/2" (1.3 cm) on one continuous edge of the band.

CONTINUED

How to Sew a BANDED TABLECLOTH

CONTINUED

----

12 Pin the right side of the opposite (unpressed) band edge to the wrong side of the center panel, aligning the raw edges and matching the dots to the seam intersections. Stitch ½" (1.3 cm) seam on each side, pivoting at each corner dot, and removing pins as you come to them.

13 Press the seam allowances toward the band. Turn the band to the right side of the tablecloth so the inner fold just covers the stitching line. The band should be an even width without ripples. Pin it in place along the inner fold. Press a crease in the outer fold.

14 *Edgestitch* close to the inner fold, removing pins as you come to them and pivoting at the corners.

QUICK REFERENCE

Edgestitch. Align the presser foot so that the needle will enter the fabric as close as possible to the folded edge. Note the point on the presser foot that aligns to the fold. Then guide the fabric to pass under the foot at that point rather than watching the needle. Stitch slowly for best control.

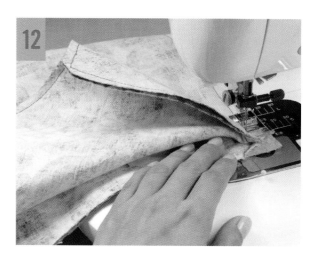

MORE IDEAS

Before pinning the band in place in step 12, page 92, center a length of jumbo rickrack over the stitching line to give your banded tablecloth a creative detail.

Make quilted placemats. Instead of welting, stitch a layer of thin polyester batting to the wrong side of the placemat top before stitching the top and bottom together. Trim the batting close to the seamline before turning the placemat right side out. Close the opening by machine and continue edgestitching, opposite, around the entire placemat. Then stitch diagonal lines across the placemat in both directions.

Make napkins with frayed edges. Set your machine for a narrow zigzag stitch, 2 mm long. Stitch 1/2" (1.3 cm) from the edge around the napkin, pivoting 1/2" (1.3 cm) from each corner. Then pull threads to fray the outer edges on each side, working from the cut edges up to the stitching line.

Button-tufted CUSHION

Button-tufted cushions can be custom shaped to fit chairs, benches, or window seats. They have inner cores of batting-wrapped foam and can be anchored to the furniture with fabric ties. Buttons keep the filling from shifting and accent the "stuffed" appearance of the cushion. Since tufted cushion covers are not usually removed, zippers or other closures are not necessary. Tightly woven decorator fabric with a stain-resistant finish, available in endless colors and designs, is a great choice for this project.

WHAT YOU'LL LEARN

How to make a simple foam and batting cushion and a cover to fit it

How to make ties

How to button-tuft a cushion

WHAT YOU'LL NEED

Fabric, amount determined after making pattern

Polyurethane foam (page 29), 1" (2.5 cm) thick

Polyester upholstery batting (page 27)

Thread to match

Buttons to cover (page 28); two for each button tuft

Button and carpet thread (page 28)

Long needle with a large eye

How to Sew a BUTTON-TUFTED CUSHION

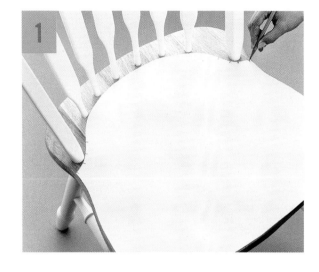

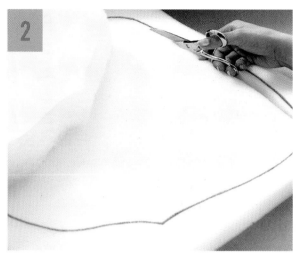

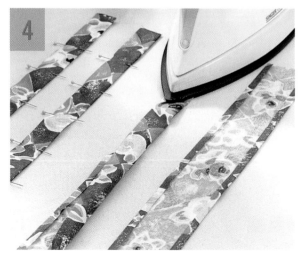

LET'S BEGIN
----

1 Make a paper pattern of the seat to be covered by the cushion, rounding any sharp corners. Simplify the shape as much as you can. Cut out the pattern and check it for *symmetry* and fit. Mark the pattern where the ties would be placed.

TIP A piece of wrapping paper or newsprint will make a sturdy pattern. You will be using this pattern for the foam, the batting, and the fabric.

2 Cut two pieces of polyester upholstery batting, using the pattern for size. Place the pattern on the foam and trace around it, using a felt-tip pen. *Cut the foam* 1/4" (6 mm) inside the marked line.

3 Place the pattern on the right side of the decorator fabric. Mark the cutting line 1" (2.5 cm) from the edge of the pattern; this allows for 1/2" (1.3 cm) **SEAM ALLOWANCES** and 1/2" (1.3 cm) for the thickness of the foam and batting. Cut the cushion top out on the marked line. Cut the cushion bottom, using the top as a pattern. Remember to *cut the covers on straight grain.* Transfer any marks for ties from the pattern to the cushion front. Omit steps 4 to 6 if your cushion will not have ties.

4 Cut two 2 1/2" × 16" (6.5 × 40.5 cm) fabric strips for each tie, following fabric grainlines. **PRESS** under 1/4" (6 mm) on the long edges of each strip. Then press them in half lengthwise, wrong sides together, aligning the pressed edges. Pin.

5 Set the machine for a straight stitch of 10 stitches per inch, which equals 2.5 mm. *Edgestitch (p. 92)* along the open edge of each tie. Leave both ends of the ties open. Tie a single knot at one end of each tie, enclosing the raw edges in the knot.

CONTINUED

QUICK REFERENCE

Symmetry. Hand-drawn patterns can easily turn out a bit askew. Fold the pattern in half to check that the edges are identical and make any necessary adjustments. Then recheck it on the seat.

Cut the foam. Polyurethane foam with a thickness of 1" (2.5 cm) can be easily cut with sewing shears. Other options include a serrated kitchen knife or an electric knife. Be sure to hold the blade perpendicular to the foam as you cut. Some fabric stores will cut the foam for you if you prepare your pattern before you go shopping.

Cut the covers on straight grain. Ideally, the center of the cushion, front to back, runs on the **LENGTHWISE GRAIN** of the fabric. If you are using a **DIRECTIONAL PRINT,** cut the pieces so the top of the design is at the back of the cushion. Center large design motifs.

How to Sew a BUTTON-TUFTED CUSHION

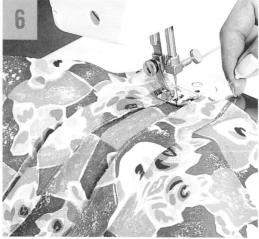

CONTINUED
---

6 Pin the unfinished ends of the ties to the right side of the cushion front at the marked positions. Stitch the ties in place 3/8" (1 cm) from the edge, *removing the pins as you come to them (p. 19)*.

TIP To make sure the ties don't get in the way when you stitch the outer seam, pin the free ends to the cushion front. Use safety pins to avoid scratching your hands when you turn the cover right side out.

7 Place the cushion top and bottom right sides together, aligning the outer edges; pin, *inserting the pins perpendicular to the edges (page 19). Leave an opening for inserting the foam*.

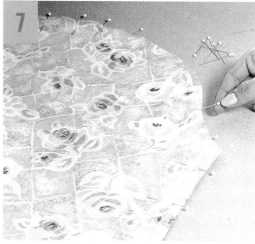

8 Place the pieces under the presser foot, just ahead of the opening. Align the cut edges to the 1/2" (1.3 cm) *seam allowance guide (p. 19)*. Remove the pin that marks the opening before lowering the presser foot.

9 *Backstitch (p. 19)* three or four stitches; stop. Then, stitching forward, stitch the seam on all sides. End the seam at the opposite side of the opening; backstitch three or four stitches.

QUICK REFERENCE

Leave an opening for inserting the foam. The size of the opening depends on the size of the cushion. For chair seats, leave at least 8" (20.5 cm) at the back of the cushion; for longer cushions, leave an entire short end open.

Clip the seam allowance. Before turning a curved seam right side out, clip the seam allowance perpendicular to the stitches every ¼" to ½" (6 mm to 1.3 cm). This allows the seam to open up for pressing or to lie along the edge without any bubbles or folds. Clip up to, but not through, the stitches. The sharper the curve, the closer together the clips should be.

Turn back the top seam allowance. It is difficult to fit a seam roll or hard cardboard tube into a cushion cover to press the seam allowances open. Turning back and pressing one seam allowance helps to separate them and make the seam look neater from the right side.

10 *Clip the seam allowances* of any curved areas. Press the seam flat. *Turn back the top seam allowance*, and press, using light pressure with the tip of your iron down the crease of the seam. Press back ½" (1.3 cm) seam allowance on the cushion cover back in the open area.

11 Reach in through the opening to turn the cushion cover completely right side out. Press lightly, centering the seam around the outer edge. Make sure the ties are sewn securely into the seam at the correct positions.

CONTINUED

How to Sew a BUTTON-TUFTED CUSHION

CONTINUED

12 Place the foam between the layers of upholstery batting. Hand-stitch the edges of the batting together, encasing the foam.

13 Fold the batted foam in half and insert it into the cushion cover. Unfold the foam, smoothing the fabric over the batting. Slipstitch (page 38) the opening closed. You can use your cushion like this if you prefer. However, if you want to add button tufting, continue with the next steps.

14 *Mark the button placement* on both sides of the cushion. Follow the manufacturer's directions for making covered buttons and the general guidelines on page 28. You will need two buttons for every tuft.

15 Cut two or three 18" (46 cm) strands of button and carpet thread (page 28); insert all the strands through the button shank, and secure at the middle of the thread with a double knot.

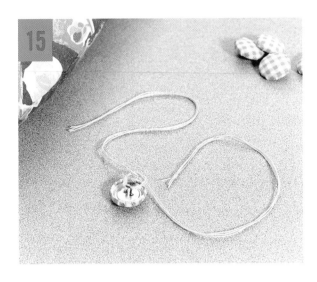

QUICK REFERENCE

Mark the button placement. Button placements are usually equally spaced in all directions. Use the pattern piece to plan out the placement, trying different arrangements. A chair seat, for instance, can have four buttons arranged in a square or a fifth button in the center.

16 Insert the ends of the thread strands through the eye of a long needle. Insert the needle through the cushion to the back side. Remove the strands from the needle and divide them into two groups.

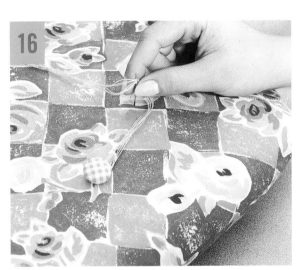

17 Thread a second button onto one group of threads. Tie a single knot, using both thread groups; pull the strands until the buttons are tight against the cushion, creating an indentation. Wrap the thread two or three times around the button shank and tie a double knot. Trim the thread tails so they are hidden under the button, but not so short that the knot could loosen. Repeat steps 15 to 17 for each tuft, keeping the indentations equal.

TIP A drop of liquid fray preventer (page 25) on the double knots would secure them permanently.

MORE IDEAS

Sew welting to the cushion front piece before adding ties or sewing it to the back. Follow pages 81 to 83, steps 4 to 10. (top left)

Sew pregathered ruffles or eyelet trim to the cushion front piece before sewing it to the back. Begin and end the trim at the ties, avoiding the cushion back. (top middle)

Make a removable cushion cover by eliminating the button tufting and adding a zipper along a straight side of the cushion. Follow the directions for zipper application on pages 118 to 121. (top right)

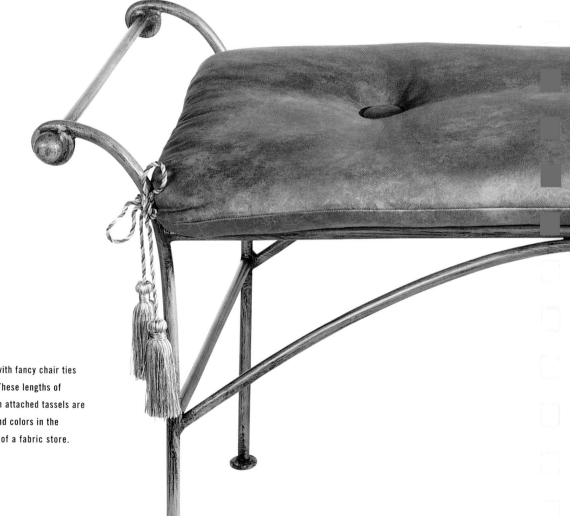

Sew elegant cushions with fancy chair ties instead of fabric ties. These lengths of decorative cording with attached tassels are found in many styles and colors in the decorator department of a fabric store.

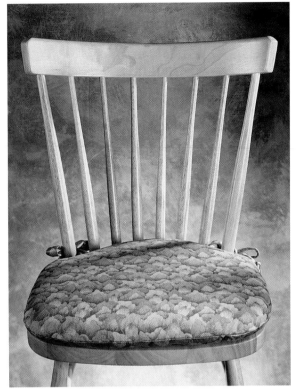

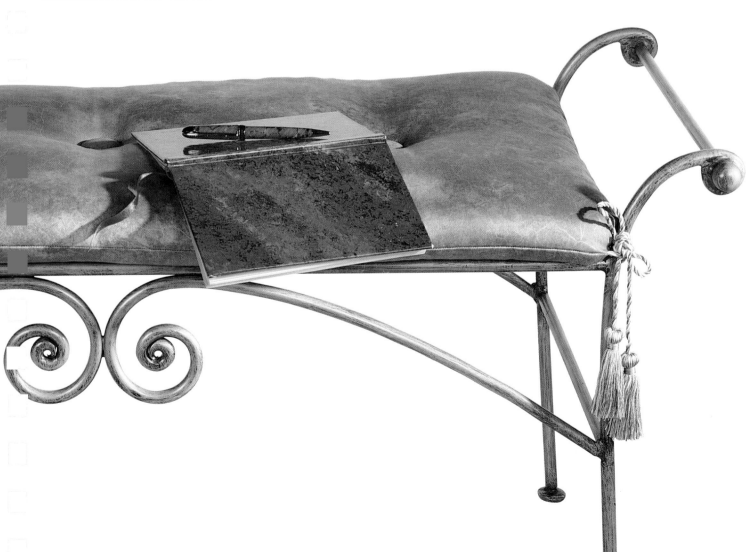

Reversible SEET COVERS

Simple seat covers give your dining room or kitchen chairs a fresh look. These **LINED-TO-THE-EDGE** covers are made with two coordinating decorator fabrics, so they can be flipped over for an instant décor change. **DARTS** sewn at the front corners shape the covers to fit the chair seats smoothly. The back corners are held in place with a button tab that wraps around the back of the leg. These covers are suitable for armless chairs that have open backs and smooth, straight sides and fronts. Because the amount of fabric needed depends on your chair size and the fabric design size, it is a good idea to make the pattern first and take it with you when you shop for fabric.

WHAT YOU'LL LEARN

How to make a muslin pattern

How to center a fabric design on your project

How to sew darts

How to sew sharp inner corners

How to make buttonholes

WHAT YOU'LL NEED

¾ yd. (0.7 m) muslin for making a pattern

Two coordinating decorator fabrics, such as a print and a stripe; amount depends on chair size and fabric design size

Thread to blend with the fabrics

Four buttons for each cover, ⅞" to 1" (2.2 to 2.5 cm) in diameter

½ yd. (0.5 m) grosgrain ribbon, ⅞" (23 mm) wide, in a color to match the fabrics

Hand-sewing needle

How to Sew a REVERSIBLE SEAT COVER

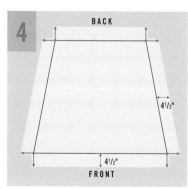

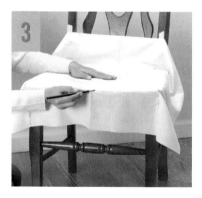

BACK

4¹/₂"

4¹/₂"

FRONT

4

LET'S BEGIN

1 Measure the chair seat side to side and front to back. Add 10" (25.5 cm) in each direction. *Cut or tear* a **MUSLIN** square to this size to make a pattern. Press the muslin pattern in half in both directions. Unfold. Center the pattern on the chair seat, allowing it to fall down over the front and sides. At the back, turn the pattern up along the legs. If necessary, tape the pattern in place.

2 Mark a dot at one front corner. Pinch the fabric together from the dot down, bringing the front to meet the side. Pin out the excess fabric, inserting the pins parallel to the chair leg, forming a dart. Mark lines on both sides of the dart from the dot down to the bottom. Repeat on the other front corner.

3 Mark dots at the back of the seat, at the inside front corners of the chair legs. (If your chair legs are round, mark each dot at a point in line with the front and side of the leg.) Trace the outline of the chair seat on the pattern.

4 Remove the pattern from the chair; remove the pins. Draw lines 4¹/₂" (11.5 cm) outside the traced seat lines. At the back corners, draw lines from the dots to the outer lines, forming squares. (These will be stitching lines.) Mark **PIVOT** points (shown in blue) on the stitching lines ¹/₂" (1.3 cm) from the outer edge. Draw cutting lines (shown in red) ¹/₂" (1.3 cm) outside the stitching lines at the legs and at the front darts. Fold the pattern in half to make sure it is symmetrical, and make any necessary corrections. Cut out the pattern on the outer lines.

5 Place the pattern on the printed (top) fabric, aligning the front-to-back crease with the **LENGTHWISE GRAIN** and the side-to-side crease with the **CROSSWISE GRAIN**. Position the pattern so that the intersection of the creases is at the exact *center of a design motif.* Cut out the seat cover top. *Transfer the pivot points and dart dots to the wrong side of the fabric.*

6 Cut out the remaining seat cover tops, using the first piece as a guide. This will make it easier to center the design motifs. Place each of the tops on the bottom fabric, right sides together. Pin near the outer edges. Cut them out; remove the pins.

7 Fold the dart on one front corner, right sides together, aligning the raw edges. Pin together, *inserting pins perpendicular to the edges (p. 19)*. Place the fabric under the presser foot, aligning the cut edges to the ½" (1.3 cm) *seam allowance guide (p. 19)*, with the open end of the dart under the presser foot. Set the machine for a straight stitch of 12 stitches per inch, which equals 2 mm. *Backstitch (p. 19)* to the end. Then stitch forward, *removing the pins as you come to them (p. 19)*. Stitch to the edge of the fold, and back-stitch a few stitches. *Remove the fabric from the machine (p. 19)*.

CONTINUED

CONTINUED

QUICK REFERENCE

Cut or tear. Muslin is an inexpensive cotton fabric. If you make a small cut in the selvage and pull it apart, it will easily tear in a straight line across the fabric. You will have to cut again at the other selvage. Then repeat the procedure in the other direction to tear it to the desired size.

Center of a design motif. The designs of a decorator fabric are printed at regularly repeating intervals lengthwise and crosswise. For best results, you should center a design motif on each of the chair seat covers. Depending on the size of the design, you will probably be wasting some fabric. It is a good idea to make the pattern before you buy the fabric, and take the pattern along so you'll know exactly how much to buy.

Transfer the pivot points and dart dots to the wrong side of the fabric. Run a pin through each dot from the right side of the pattern. On the back side of the cover fabric, where the pins exit, mark the dots using pencil, chalk, or fabric marker.

How to Sew a REVERSIBLE SEAT COVER

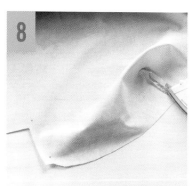

CONTINUED

----

8 Repeat step 7 for the remaining front corners on the top and bottom pieces. **PRESS** the seam allowances of the darts open.

TIP When you press the dart seam allowances open, the fabric at the end of the dart will fold down in a triangle shape, with the top of the triangle at the tip of the dart. Hold the corner so the right side of the dart is flat on the pressing surface. Press the triangle flat, using the tip of the iron.

9 Place the top and bottom seat covers right sides together aligning the raw edges; pin. Align the seams of the front darts, *inserting pins in the wells of the seams.* Place the fabric under the presser foot near the center of the back edge, so that the cut edges are aligned to the 1/2" (1.3 cm) seam allowance guide. Backstitch a few stitches. Then stitch forward, guiding the cut edges along the 1/2" (1.3 cm) seam allowance guide. Remove the pins as you come to them.

10 Stop stitching at the first corner, leaving the needle down in the fabric. (Turn the hand-wheel until the needle is down.) Raise the presser foot, and turn the fabric. Lower the presser foot, and continue. **PIVOT** in the same way at each corner. Stop stitching about 6" (15 cm) from where you began; backstitch a few stitches. This leaves an opening for turning the cover right side out.

11 *Trim the seam allowances diagonally (p. 51)* at the outer corners. *Clip to, but not through (p. 67)* the stitches at the inner corners

12 *Turn back the top seam allowance and press (p. 99),* applying light pressure with the tip of the iron down the crease of the seam. In the area of the opening, turn back and press the seam allowances 1/2" (1.3 cm).

13 Turn the cover right side out through the opening. Insert a point turner or similar tool into the opening and gently push the pivot points out to form *perfect corners (p. 51).* Push the seam out so that it is centered all around the outer edge; press. Align the folded edges of the opening and pin them closed. *Edgestitch (p. 92)* around the seat cover, stitching the opening closed; pivot at the corners. Overlap the stitches about 1/2" (1.3 cm) where they meet.

14 Mark placement lines for the buttonholes parallel to and 1" (2.5 cm) above the lower side edges. Mark lines that equal the diameter plus the thickness of the buttons, with one end 1" (2.5 cm) from the vertical edges. Attach your buttonhole presser foot or buttonhole attachment. Follow the instructions in your owner's manual to stitch the buttonholes over the marked lines. Apply liquid fray preventer (page 25) to the buttonholes; allow it to dry. Cut the buttonholes open, using a buttonhole cutter or small, sharp scissors.

💡

QUICK REFERENCE

Inserting pins in the wells of the seams. By pinning the darts together with a pin directly in the center of the seamlines, you are making sure that the darts will line up perfectly on the right side of the cover. Stitch up to these pins as close as you can before removing them.

15 Place the cover on the chair seat. At the back of one chair leg, measure the distance between buttonholes. Cut ribbon 4" (10 cm) longer than this measurement. Turn under 1" (2.5 cm) on each end of the ribbon; press. Turn the raw ends under again, aligning them to the pressed folds and encasing the raw edges. Stitch across the inner folds, forming *double-fold hems (p. 45)*. Hand-stitch a button (page 39) to the center of each hem. Repeat for the other leg. Button the chair seat cover in place.

Synthetic Fleece THROW

When there's a chill in the air, you'll be cuddled up cozy in your synthetic fleece throw. Not just for cold-weather climates, synthetic fleece is a comfortable choice for cool southern mornings and evenings, too. The contemporary flowers are raw-edge **APPLIQUÉS** with fleece pompom centers. Because the cut edges of synthetic fleece don't ravel, a throw requires very little sewing, and edges can simply be cut into fringe.

WHAT YOU'LL LEARN

How to use a rotary cutter and mat

How to sew raw-edge appliqués

Quick and easy tricks for cutting fringe

Synthetic fleece might be your new favorite fabric

WHAT YOU'LL NEED

2 yd. (1.85 m) polyester fleece for the throw

¼ yd. (0.25 m) fleece for flower appliqués

⅛ yd. (0.15 m) fleece for flower centers

Paper for drawing the appliqué pattern

Rotary cutter and mat

Metal or heavy plastic straightedge

Temporary fabric adhesive

Narrow masking tape; pencil

Thread to match the fabrics

4" (10 cm) square of cardboard

How to Sew a SYNTHETIC FLEECE THROW

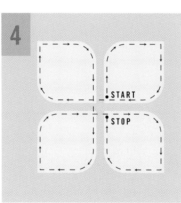

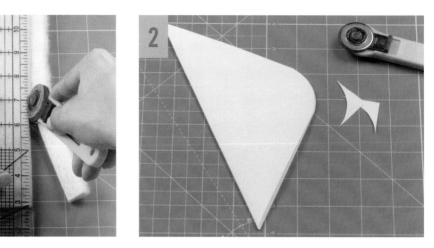

3 Position the flowers in blocks of four petals each, with the square corners at the centers and outer edges of the flowers. Space the petals evenly 3/8" (1 cm) apart. Spray the wrong side of the petals with **TEMPORARY FABRIC ADHESIVE**, following the manufacturer's directions. Adhere them in place.

TIP To protect your work surface from overspray, place the pieces in the bottom of a box.

4 Insert a ballpoint or universal point needle into the machine (page 10). Wind a bobbin with thread to match the throw fabric, and insert it into the machine. Thread the upper machine with a color that matches the petals. *Edgestitch (p. 92)* around petals of one flower in one continuous stitching line, beginning at the center point of one petal. Stitch slowly around the curves, stopping and turning fabric as needed. **PIVOT** fabric at the square corners. Overlap a few stitches where they meet. Repeat for each of the flowers.

LET'S BEGIN

---

1 Square off the ends of the fleece and trim off the **SELVAGES**, using a *rotary cutter and mat (p. 23)* with a metal or heavy plastic straightedge.

2 Cut out a 5" (12.7 cm) paper square for the appliqué pattern. Fold it in half diagonally, and round the two open corners. Unfold. Using the pattern, cut out 12 flower petals from the appliqué fleece.

TIP By threading the machine in this way, the stitches will be less visible on both sides of the throw. They will simply sink into the fleece. The back of the throw will look as if it has been quilted.

5 Place a strip of narrow masking tape 5" (12.7 cm) from one end of the throw. Mark the tape every ½" (1.3 cm). Using a rotary cutter and mat and a straightedge, cut fabric perpendicular to the tape at each mark, fringing the edge. Remove the tape. Repeat at the other end. Tie a knot at the top of each fringe strip, tying all of them in the same direction for best appearance.

TIP You may be able to use the same strip of tape on the opposite end. It only has to be slightly sticky to serve its purpose.

6 Cut the pompom fabric into four ½" × 30" (1.3 × 76 cm) strips on the crosswise grain; trim off the selvages at the ends. Stretch the strips to make them curl. Cut one of the strips into three pieces for the ties.

7 Wrap a long strip around a 4" (10 cm) square of cardboard. Slide the loops off the cardboard and tie them around the center with a short strip forming a pompom. Cut the loops, if desired. Repeat to make the other pompoms. Trim the tie ends to the same length as the other pieces. Hand-stitch a pompom to the center of each flower.

QUICK REFERENCE

Rotary cutter and mat. These time-saving tools for cutting fabric may take a little practice and serious precautions. The blade on a rotary cutter is extremely sharp. Cut slowly, guiding the blade along the straightedge. Watch your fingers, and always retract or cover the blade between cuts. The rotary cutter cannot be used without the special protective mat.

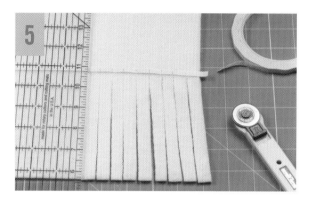

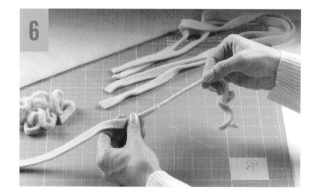

Knife-edge PILLOWS

The knife-edge pillow is probably the most versatile style for decorating your home. There are no limits to the variations you can create, not only in size, color, and texture, but also in added details that give your pillow a personal touch. The directions that follow are for a knife-edge pillow that is 14" (35.5 cm) square. For your first knife-edge pillow, we recommend a firmly woven mediumweight fabric.

Ready-made knife-edge pillow inserts come in a wide selection of sizes, including 12", 14", 16", 18", 20", 24", and 30" (30.5, 35.5, 40.5, 46, 51, 61, and 76 cm) squares and a 12" × 16" (30.5 × 40.5 cm) rectangle. By adapting these cutting instructions, you can sew a cover for any size pillow insert. You can also use these instructions to sew your own pillow inserts in any size you like, stuffing them to a plumpness that pleases you.

WHAT YOU'LL LEARN

How to backstitch

How to set and PRESS seams

Tricks for sewing
perfect corners

How to slipstitch an opening
closed by hand

WHAT YOU'LL NEED

14" (35.5 cm) square
pillow form

½ yd. (0.5 m) of fabric

Matching thread

Hand-sewing needle

Sewing PROJECTS

How to Sew a KNIFE-EDGE PILLOW

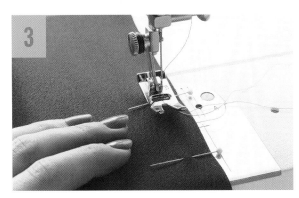

1 Cut two 15" (38 cm) squares of fabric, aligning the sides to the fabric **GRAINLINES**. A ½" (1.3 cm) **SEAM ALLOWANCE** is needed on each side, so 1" (2.5 cm) is added to each dimension of the *desired finished size.*

2 Place the pillow front over the pillow back, right sides together, and align all four edges. Pin the layers together near the outer edges, *inserting the pins perpendicular to the edges (p. 19).* In the center of one side, leave a 7" (18 cm) opening unpinned.

3 Place the fabric under the presser foot, just ahead of the opening. Align the cut edges of the fabric to the ½" (1.3 cm) *seam allowance guide (p. 19)* on the bed of your machine. Remove the pin that marks the opening, before lowering the presser foot.

4 *Backstitch (p. 19)* three or four stitches; stop. Then, stitching forward, stitch the seam on all four sides, **PIVOTING** with the needle down at the corners. End the **SEAM** at the opposite side of the opening; backstitch three or four stitches.

5 *Remove the fabric from the machine (p. 19).* Trim the threads close to the fabric. Press the seams flat to set the stitching line in the fabric. This may seem unnecessary, but it really does give you a better-looking seam in the end.

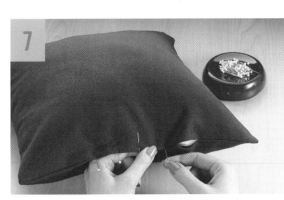

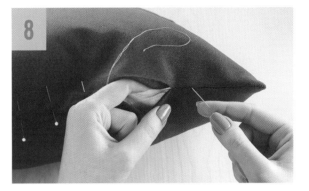

6 Turn back the top seam allowance and press, applying light pressure with tip of the iron down the crease of the seam. In the area of the opening, turn back and press the top seam allowance 1/2" (1.3 cm). Turn the cover over; turn back and press the remaining opening seam allowance.

7 Turn the pillow cover right side out through the opening. Compress and insert the pillow form. Align the pressed edges of the opening, and pin the opening closed. Thread a hand needle and tie a knot in the end.

8 Slipstitch the opening closed, following the instructions on page 38.

QUICK REFERENCE

Desired finished size. To make a knife-edge pillow of a different size, simply cut your fabric 1" (2.5 cm) larger in both directions than the desired finished size of your pillow. Cut 17" (43 cm) squares for a 16" (40.5 cm) pillow; cut 13" × 19" (33 × 48.5 cm) rectangles for a 12" × 18" (30.5 × 46 cm) pillow.

How to Sew a KNIFE-EDGE PILLOW

ALTERNATE STEPS FOR A ZIPPER CLOSURE

LET'S BEGIN
----

1 Place the pillow front over the pillow back, right sides together. Pin the side that will have the zipper. Center the zipper alongside the pinned edges, and mark the **SEAM ALLOWANCES** just above and below the *zipper stops.*

TIP For best results, select a side that was cut on the **LENGTHWISE GRAIN** of the fabric. The lengthwise grain is more stable and will have less tendency to stretch as you sew.

2 Stitch a ½" (1.3 cm) **SEAM** from the upper edge to the mark, *backstitching (p. 19)* at the beginning and the end. Repeat at the lower edge. Leave the center section open.

3 *Machine-baste (p. 55)* on the seamline between the marks. Clip the basting stitches every 2" (5 cm) with a seam ripper (page 25). This will make the stitches easier to remove later.

4 **PRESS** the seam flat; then press the seam allowances open. *Finish the raw edges (p. 59)* with a **ZIGZAG** stitch.

TIP If your fabric is loosely woven or tends to ravel easily, repeated washings could make the seam allowances ravel away and ruin your pillow. As a preventative measure, take the time to finish all of the seam allowances.

5 Apply basting tape (page 26) to the right side of the zipper tape, running it along both outer edges.

CONTINUED

💡

QUICK REFERENCE

Zipper stops. Tiny metal bars are attached to the top and bottom of the zipper coil to prevent the zipper slide from sliding right off the end. On a conventional zipper, there is one wide stop at the bottom of the zipper and separate smaller stops at the top.

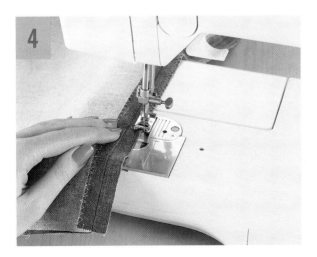

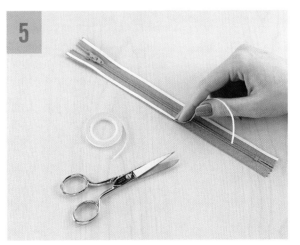

How to Sew a ZIPPER CLOSURE

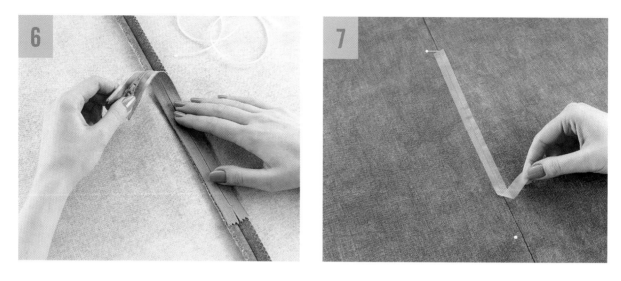

CONTINUED

6 Place the zipper facedown over the seam, with the zipper coil directly over the basted part of the seamline and the pull tab turned down. The zipper coil should be centered between the backstitched areas. Press with your fingers to secure the zipper to the seam allowances.

7 Spread the pillow pieces flat, right side up. Insert pins in the seamline, just above and below the zipper stops. Cut 1/2" (1.3 cm) transparent tape to fit between the pins; place it down the center of the seamline.

8 Attach the zipper foot and adjust it to the left of the needle. If your zipper foot is not adjustable, adjust the needle to the right of the foot. Stitch along the outer edge of the tape, stitching across one end, down one side, and across the other end; **PIVOT** at the corners.

9 Adjust the zipper foot to the right of the needle or adjust your needle to the left of the foot. Stitch over the previous stitches at one end, down the opposite side, and over the stitches at the other end. Clip the threads.

10 Remove the tape. Carefully remove the machine basting in the seamline, using a seam ripper.

11 Open the zipper. Pin the pillow front and back, right sides together, along the three remaining sides. Stitch 1/2" (1.3 cm) seam; press. Turn the pillow cover right side out and insert the pillow form through the zipper opening.

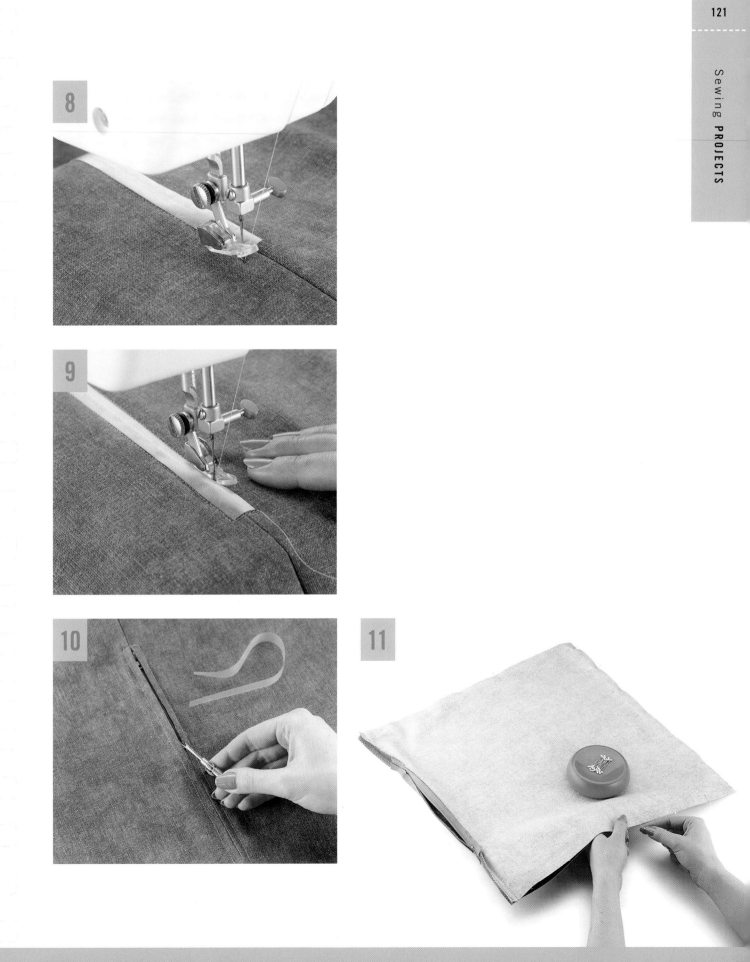

Nine-patch PILLOWS

Stitch nine squares of fabric together in a checkerboard pattern to create this interesting pillow top. Select two medium-weight fabrics that coordinate with each other; two prints, a print and a solid color, or two solids. Use one of the fabrics for the pillow back and five small squares; use the other fabric for the remaining four squares.

How to Sew a NINE-PATCH PILLOW

1 Cut a 19" (48.5 cm) square of fabric A for the pillow back. From the remaining fabric, cut five 7" (18 cm) squares. Cut four 7" (18 cm) squares from fabric B.

2 Pin one A square to one B square along one side, right sides together; align the cut ends and edges. Place the fabric under the presser foot, with the upper edges even with the needle hole in the throat plate. Align the cut edges of the fabric to the 1/2" (1.3 cm), *seam allowance guide (p. 19)* on the bed of your machine. Stitch 1/2" (1.3 cm) **SEAM**, *removing pins as you come to them (p. 19)*.

3 Pin another A square to the opposite side of the B square. Stitch 1/2" (1.3 cm) seam, forming a three-square strip. Repeat steps 2 and 3 to make another identical three-square strip. Then join the remaining three squares with an A square in the center. This will be the center strip.

4 **PRESS** all the seams flat to set the stitches. Then press the seams open. The strips should now measure 7" × 19" (18 × 48.5 cm).

5 Pin the top strip to the center strip, with right sides together and raw edges even. Align the seams, *inserting pins in the wells of the seams (p. 109)*. Stitch ¹/₂" (1.3 cm) seam, removing pins as you come to them. Be sure that **SEAM ALLOWANCES** remain open as they were pressed.

TIP Slow your stitching as you approach each seam. Stopping with the needle down in the fabric, raise the presser foot. Lift the strips slightly from the machine bed, to be sure that the seam allowance on the underside is still open and lying flat. Then lower the presser foot and continue sewing across the seam.

6 Pin the remaining strip to the opposite side of the center strip, pinning as in step 5; stitch a ¹/₂" (1.3 cm) seam. Press the seam allowances flat; then press them open. Complete the pillow, following steps 2 through 8 on pages 116 and 117. Or, if you prefer, follow the directions for a zipper closure (page 118).

Harem PILLOWS

A harem pillow is really a basic knife-edge pillow with simple shaping at the corners to give it softness and depth. This floor pillow can be stuffed with a 24" (61 cm) pillow form. Or you can easily adapt the instructions to cover pillow forms in any size for your bed, sofa, and floor. Select an easy-care fabric that is also comfortable and durable. Because floor pillows get a lot of use and may require occasional cleaning, consider sewing the cover with a zipper closure, as on page 118.

WHAT YOU'LL LEARN

How to gather fabric

How to save many decorating dollars by making your own floor pillows

WHAT YOU'LL NEED

1½ yd. (1.4 m) fabric, 45" (115 cm) wide or ¾ yd. (0.7 m) fabric, 54" to 60" (137 to 152.5 cm) wide

Thread to match the fabric

24" (61 cm) square pillow form

Hand-sewing needle

How to Sew a HAREM PILLOW

1 Cut two 25" (63.5 cm) squares of fabric for the front and back of the pillow. Follow steps 2 to 7 on pages 116 and 117, for a pillow with a slip-stitched closure. Leave a 12" (30.5 cm) opening. Or follow steps 1 to 11 on pages 118 to 121 for a pillow with a zipper closure, leaving the pillow inside out.

2 Mark points 3" (7.5 cm) from a corner along each seam-line. Draw a diagonal line, connecting the points. Repeat this at each corner.

TIP Harem pillows can be made in any size. For pillows 16" (40.5 cm) or smaller, measure 2" (5 cm) from the corners.

3 Thread a needle with regular thread and knot the two ends together so you have a doubled thread. Insert the needle into the fabric near the cut edge and on the diagonal line. Pass the needle through the loop of the doubled thread just before the knot, and pull it taut. Hand-baste along the line with 1/4" (6 mm) running stitches for gathering.

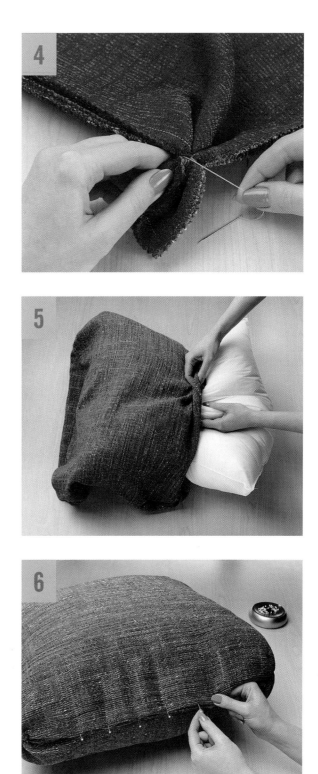

4 Pull the doubled thread to gather the corner tight. Wrap the thread several times around the corner. Secure thread with a knot or several small stitches.

5 Repeat steps 3 and 4 at each corner. Turn the pillow right side out through the opening. Insert the pillow form.

6 Pin the opening closed. Slipstitch the opening as on page 38. Or, zip the pillow closed.

Mock Box PILLOWS

For a soft, chunky look, make mock box pillows. Simply modify the corners of a basic knife-edge pillow to give it a deeper, more squared appearance. Any size pillow will work. Keep in mind that when you square off the corners to increase the depth, the outer dimensions get slightly smaller. Use a pillow form the same size as the knife-edge pillow before squaring the corners.

As a bit of a challenge, we have designed this pillow from striped fabric. You will be able to match up the stripes, making them run continuously around the pillow, as long as the two pieces you cut are identical.

WHAT YOU'LL LEARN

How to match stripes

How to sew square corners

WHAT YOU'LL NEED

⅝ yd. (0.6 m) striped fabric

Thread to match the fabric

Square pillow form

Hand-sewing needle

How to Sew a MOCK BOX PILLOW

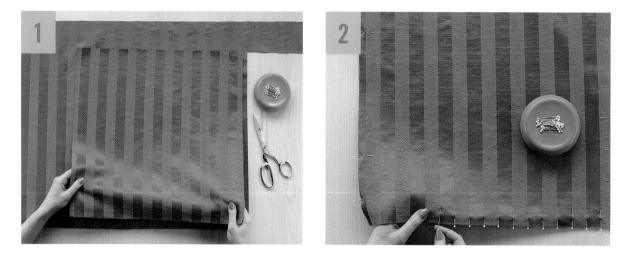

LET'S BEGIN

1 Cut two identical squares of fabric for the front and back of the pillow. The easiest way to do this is to cut the front first, and then use it as a pattern to cut the back, aligning the stripes.

2 Pin the pillow front to the pillow back, right sides together, *inserting pins perpendicular to the edges (p. 19)*. Pin frequently along the edges where the stripes match up, inserting the pins through matching points in the stripes along the 1/2" (1.3 cm) seamline. Leave an opening for turning on a side where you do not have to match up stripes.

3 Follow steps 3 to 6 on pages 116 to 117 for a knife-edge pillow. Stitch slowly on the sides where stripes match up, stitching up close to each pin before removing it.

4 Separate the front and back at one corner. Center the **SEAMS** on each side of the corner, pinning through the seams to make sure they are aligned.

5 Measure along the seam and mark a point 2" (5 cm) from the corner. Draw a line, through the mark perpendicular to the seam, from fold to fold. This will give you a corner depth of 4" (10 cm).

TIP The distance you measure along the seam is equal to half the depth of the corner. So, if you want a depth of 3" (7.5 cm), measure 1 1/2" (3.8 cm) from the corner; if you want a depth of 3 1/2" (9 cm), measure 1 3/4" (4.5 cm) from the corner.

6 Stitch on the marked line, *backstitching (p. 19)* at the beginning and end. Do not trim the seam.

7 Repeat steps 4 to 6 at each corner. Turn the pillow cover right side out. Insert the pillow form, and slipstitch the opening closed (page 38).

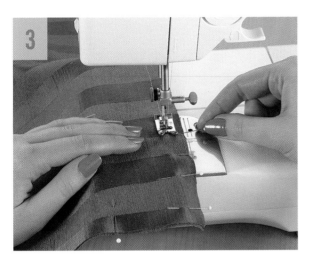

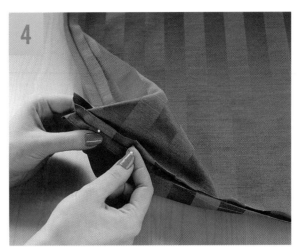

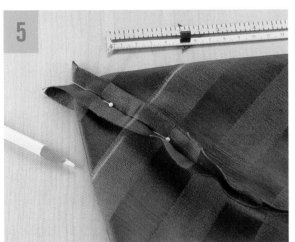

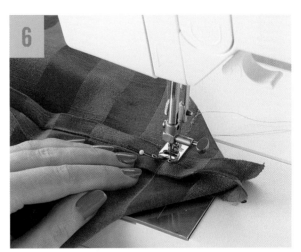

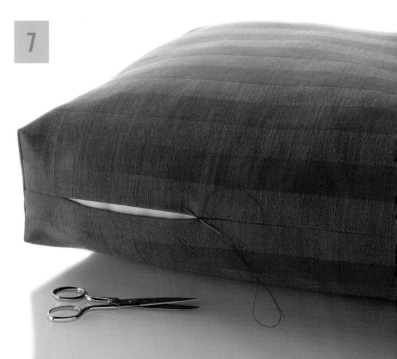

Decorator PILLOWS

Designer pillows are often expensive, but with a small amount of fabric and an interesting trim, you can create your own personally designed one-of-a-kind pillow. Choose complementary patterns and colors in mediumweight fabrics to make handsome decorator accents for your home. Because only a small amount of each fabric is required, check the remnant bins for some bargain-priced great finds.

These directions are for an 18" (46 cm) pillow, but you could easily adapt them for any size pillow. Simply graph out the pillow size you want, planning the center panel to measure about two-thirds of the total size. Add 1/2" (1.3 cm) **SEAM ALLOWANCE** to the outer edge of each piece.

How to Sew a DECORATOR PILLOW

1 Mark and cut one 13" (33 cm) square of fabric for the front center panel. Remember to trim away the **SELVAGE** and follow the **GRAINLINES**. Mark and cut a 19" (48.5 cm) square for the pillow back. Then mark and cut two rectangles each 4" × 13" (10 × 33 cm) and two rectangles each 4" × 19" (10 × 48.5 cm), for the front border strips.

2 Pin one 13" (33 cm) border strip to the upper edge of the center panel with the right sides together, aligning the cut edges. *Insert the pins perpendicular to the edges (p. 19).* Pin the other 13" (33 cm) strip to the lower edge of the center panel in the same way.

3 Set your machine for a straight stitch of 10 stitches per inch, which equals 2.5 mm. Place the upper pinned edges under the presser foot, aligning them to the ½" (1.3 cm) *seam allowance guide (p. 19).* Stitch the ½" (1.3 cm) **SEAM**, *backstitching (p. 19)* at the beginning and end of the seam. *Remove the pins as you come to them (p. 19).* Stitch the lower seam in the same way.

4 **PRESS** over the stitching lines of the closed seams to set the stitches in the fabric. Then open the seam allowances and press them again.

5 Cut two 13" (33 cm) strips of decorator trim. Center a strip over each seamline. Hold the trim in place with the glue stick adhesive.

6 Stitch each trim in place, stitching along the outer edge of one side and then the other. Stitch in the same direction on both sides to keep the trim from puckering. Make sure the seam allowances on the underside remain open.

 TIP Keep the trim strips "relaxed" as you position them in place. Stretching them will cause your fabric to pucker after stitching.

CONTINUED

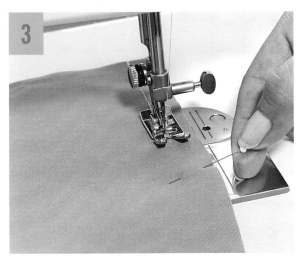

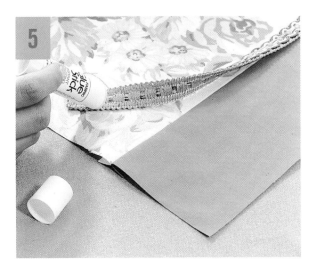

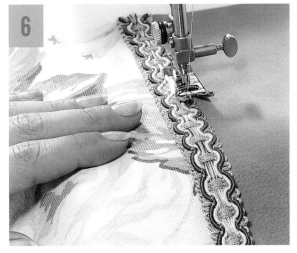

How to Sew a DECORATOR PILLOW

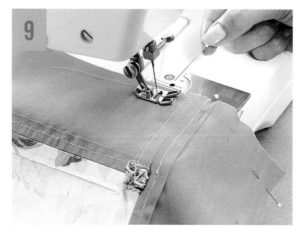

7 Pin the two 19" (48.5 cm) border strips to the sides of the front pillow section, right sides together. Stitch 1/2" (1.3 cm) seams, sewing slowly through the areas where you cross the previous seams. Repeat steps 4 to 6 for the new seams to complete the pillow front. If you want to sew a zipper closure, complete your pillow following steps 1 to 11, pages 118 to 121.

8 Place the pillow front over the pillow back, right sides together, and align the four outer edges. Pin them together, inserting the pins perpendicular to the edges. In the center of the bottom, leave a 9" (23 cm) opening unpinned. Mark dots 1/2" (1.3 cm) from each corner.

9 Place the fabric under the presser foot, just ahead of the opening. Align the cut edges to the 1/2" (1.3 cm) seam allowance guide. Remove the pin that marks the opening, before lowering the presser foot.

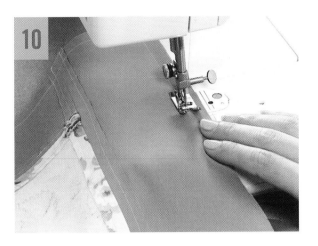

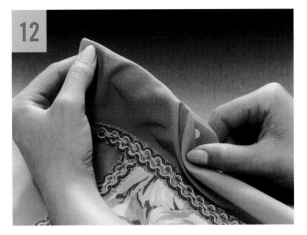

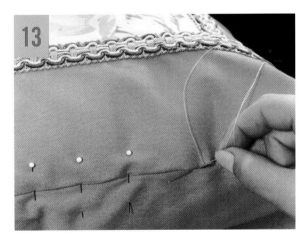

10 Backstitch three or four stitches; stop. Then, stitching forward, stitch the seam on all four sides, **PIVOTING** on the dots, with the needle down in the fabric at each corner. End the seam at the opposite side of the opening; backstitch three or four stitches.

11 Press the seam flat. *Turn back the top seam allowance (p. 99),* and press, using light pressure with the tip of your iron down the crease of the seam.

12 Reach in through the opening to grasp a corner and pull it out through the opening. Repeat with the other three corners to turn the pillow completely right side out. Use a point turner or similar tool to create *perfect corners (p. 51).*

13 Compress and insert the pillow form through the opening. Manipulate the form into the corners of the pillow. Slipstitch the opening closed, following the directions on page 38.

MORE IDEAS

Introduce a third fabric in
the border. Sew a set
of pillows, rearranging the
placement of the fabrics
in each one.

Sew a decorator pillow that
showcases a piece of needlework in the center square.
Accent the border seams with
flat lace trim or ribbon.

For an interesting tone-
on-tone effect, select a
reversible jacquard fabric.
Use one side up for
the center square and the
opposite side up for
the border.

Eliminate trims, and
hand-stitch large decorative
buttons to the corners of the
center square before
inserting the pillow form.
Sew tassels to the corners.

Envelope PILLOWS

This unique pillow cover is made from a single rectangle of fabric that wraps around the pillow form. One end, stitched to create a triangular flap, is secured with a button. The other end of the rectangle is folded inside the finished pillow and encloses the form to keep it neatly hidden. The pillow form is easily removed when you want to clean the pillow cover. For economical use of fabric yardage, cut the long rectangle on the **CROSSWISE GRAIN** of the fabric. Select fabric carefully. Suitable fabrics include stripes that run on the crosswise grain, solid colors, and small nondirectional prints. Avoid **DIRECTIONAL PRINTS** and stripes that run on the **LENGTHWISE GRAIN.**

The following directions are for a 16" (40.5 cm) pillow, though envelope pillows can be made in any size. For a different-size pillow, cut the fabric rectangle with the length equal to two-and-one-half times the size of the pillow form plus 6½" (16.3 cm) and the width equal to the size of the pillow form plus 1" (2.5 cm).

WHAT YOU'LL LEARN

How to finish a raw fabric edge with ZIGZAG STITCHES

Stitch settings are easily changed from straight stitch to zigzag stitch

How to sew, trim, and turn a point

How to sew a buttonhole

WHAT YOU'LL NEED

½ yd. (0.5 m) of 48" to 60" (122 to 152.5 cm) fabric

Matching thread

Decorative shank button, about 1" (2.5 cm) in diameter

Small sharp scissors or seam ripper

16" (40.5 cm) pillow form

Hand-sewn needle

How to Sew an ENVELOPE PILLOW

LET'S BEGIN

1 Cut one rectangle of fabric, 46½" × 17" (118.3 × 43 cm). Draw light lines on the fabric with a fabric marker or light pencil. Or make a paper pattern first, if you prefer. Make sure the four corners of the rectangle are at right angles.

2 Fold one short end of the fabric rectangle in half, right sides together; pin. Stitch a ½" (1.3 cm) **SEAM**, *backstitching (p. 19)* at the beginning and end. This will form the triangular flap.

3 *Trim the seam allowance diagonally (p. 51)* at the folded end, trimming to within ⅛" (3 mm) of the stitches. **PRESS** the seam flat. Then press the seam allowances open.

> **TIP** Trim away slightly more than a 45-degree wedge. This will allow the point of the flap to lie flat and smooth when the fabric is turned right side out.

4 Turn the stitched flap right side out. Use a point turner or a similar tool to carefully push the point out, if necessary. Center the seam between the two long sides of the rectangle and press the diagonal folds. The seamed side of the flap is now the flap *facing*.

> **TIP** Remember that "press" means to lift the iron to move it to a new position. Avoid sliding the iron, which could cause this **BIAS** fold to stretch out of shape.

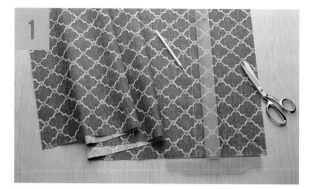

QUICK REFERENCE

Facing. This is a fabric extension or additional piece of fabric sewn as a backing to another piece to protect raw edges from raveling and give the item (in this case a pillow flap) a neat, finished appearance.

5 Set the pattern selector to **ZIGZAG** and your stitch width and length to medium. *Finish the raw edge (p. 59)* of the flap facing by zigzagging from one pressed fold, across the seam, to the opposite pressed fold. Also finish the opposite end of the rectangle with a zigzag stitch.

6 Mark a line ½" (1.3 cm) from the finished edge of the flap facing with an erasable fabric marker or chalk. Pin the flap facing to the flap as it was pressed, making sure both layers are smooth and the seam is still centered between the long sides. Insert the pins perpendicular to the marked line. Reset the pattern selector and stitch width to straight stitch settings. Stitch the facing to the flap along the marked line.

7 Fold the flap down along the stitching line; the facing will be against the wrong side of the fabric. Press along the stitching line. Pin-mark a point 6" (15 cm) from the lower edge on each long side of the rectangle. Fold the fabric, right sides together, aligning the pressed fold of the triangular flap with the pin marks.

CONTINUED

How to Sew an ENVELOPE PILLOW

8 Fold the extra 6" (15 cm) of fabric, right side down, over the triangular flap. Pin the raw edges together along both sides. Stitch ½" (1.3 cm) seams. Press the seams flat, then open.

9 Turn the pillow cover right side out. The 6" (15 cm) extension becomes an inner flap that will wrap over the top of the pillow form. Press the pillow cover.

10 Push a pin through the seamline of the triangular flap facing 1¼" (3.2 cm) from the point. Insert a second pin 1⅛" (2.8 cm) above the first one. On the right side, mark a removable line between the two pins, for the buttonhole. Stitch the buttonhole and button as in steps 12 and 13 on page 68.

TIP This buttonhole size is appropriate for a relatively flat 1" (2.5 cm) button. If you select a different-size button, the correct buttonhole length is equal to the diameter of the button plus the thickness of the button plus ⅛" (3 mm). Always make a test buttonhole on a scrap of fabric.

MORE IDEAS

Hand-stitch fringe trim along the edge of the triangular flap, turning the ends under ¾" (2 cm). Apply liquid fray preventer on the ends of the trim to prevent raveling.

Block-print fabric paint designs on the finished pillow cover before inserting the pillow form. Allow the paint to dry completely; heat-set the designs with an iron. Attach beaded dangles to a stone ring for an eye-catching closure.

Pillow CASES

Brighten up your bedding ensemble with easy-to-sew pillow cases. Choose three coordinating fabrics: one for the main body of the case, one for the contrasting **HEM** band, and a striped fabric to make a **BIAS** trim. Look for washable cotton or cotton/ polyester blend fabrics that will feel comfortable against your skin. The chart in step 1 shows the dimensions of bed pillows and the sizes to cut the pillow case body pieces for each.

WHAT YOU'LL LEARN

How to machine-baste

How to make a bias trim

How to finish raw edges with a ZIGZAG STITCH

How to encase a raw edge in a hem band

WHAT YOU'LL NEED

1¼ yd. (1.15 m) fabric for the pillow case body

³⁄₈ yd. (0.35 m) fabric for the hem band

½ yd. (0.5 m) striped fabric for the bias trim

Rotary cutter and mat, heavy plastic quilter's ruler (optional for cutting bias trim)

Thread to blend with the fabrics

How to Sew a PILLOW CASE

LET'S BEGIN
----

1 Preshrink the fabrics (page 33). Cut a rectangle of fabric for the pillow case body, according to the chart, running the longer sides parallel to the **LENGTHWISE GRAIN**. Cut a rectangle of fabric for the hem band 41" × 10" (104 × 25.5 cm), running the longer sides parallel to the **CROSSWISE GRAIN**. Do not use a **SELVAGE** as an edge.

2 Cut the selvages from the striped fabric. Place the fabric on an ironing surface. Fold the fabric diagonally, turning the left side over to align to the upper edge. The lengthwise grain of the upper layer should be parallel to the crosswise grain of the lower layer. **PRESS** the fold, *taking care not to distort it.* The foldline lies on the true bias.

3 Mark a line 2" (5 cm) from the fold. Cut both layers. Then cut this bias strip in half along the foldline.

TIP If you have a rotary cutter, cutting mat, and quilter's ruler, you can easily cut these bias strips by aligning the 45° angle line on the ruler to the fabric edge and cutting the fabric diagonally along the edge of the ruler.

4 Trim the ends of both strips parallel to the stripes. Draw a line 1/4" (6 mm) from the cut ends on the wrong side of the fabric; this will be the seamline. Place the strips, right sides together, aligning the raw edges on one end. The ends of the marked lines should align, so a small triangle of fabric extends on each side. Pin, *inserting the pins perpendicular to the edges (p. 19).* Stitch on the seam-line, *removing the pins as you come to them (p. 19).*

5 Press the seam allowances open. Trim off the triangular points. Press the bias strip in half, taking care not to distort the width of the strip. Cut the strip 41" (104 cm) long, cutting both ends straight across.

CONTINUED

1

PILLOW SIZE	CUT SIZE OF CASE BODY
Standard 20" × 26" (51 × 66 cm)	41" × 27" (104 × 68.5 cm)
Queen 20" × 30" (51 × 76 cm)	41" × 31" (104 × 78.5 cm)
King 20" × 36" (51 × 91.5 cm)	41" × 37" (104 × 94 cm)

2

3

4

5

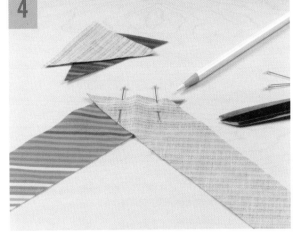

QUICK REFERENCE

Taking care not to distort it. Fabric has a lot of "give" in the bias direction, so it is easily distorted. If you simply slide the iron along the fold, it will probably grow in length and get wavy. Instead, lift and move the iron to press the fold, and continually check that to see that it lies flat.

How to Sew a PILLOW CASE

CONTINUED

---

6 Pin the bias trim to one long edge of the pillow case body. If you have selected a **DIRECTIONAL PRINT** for the body, pin the trim to the side where you want the hem. Insert the pins perpendicular to the edges, and check that the trim width is always 1" (2.5 cm). Set the machine for a long straight stitch, and **BASTE** the trim to the pillow case body, guiding the raw edges along the 3/8" (1 cm) *seam allowance guide (p. 19).* Remove pins as you come to them.

TIP If you baste the trim to the pillow case body with the trim on the underside, the trim width is less likely to become distorted. It is harder to see the pins this way, so leave the pin heads extending off the edge.

7 Press the hem in half, wrong sides together, lengthwise; unfold. Press under 1/2" (1.3 cm) on one long edge. Pin the plain edge of the hem, right side down, to the wrong side of the pillow case body. Reset the machine to a stitch length of 10 stitches per inch, which equals 2.5 mm. Stitch, guiding the raw edges along the 1/2" (1.3 cm) seam allowance guide.

8 Place the pillow case facedown on the ironing surface. Turn the hem away from the body and press along the seamline.

9 Turn the pillow case over. Turn the hem back along the foldline, just covering the inner stitching line with the folded edge of the hem. Pin. *Edgestitch (p. 92)* close to the fold, removing the pins as you come to them.

10 Fold the pillow case in half, right sides together, aligning the unfinished edges. Pin. Stitch a 1/2" (1.3 cm) seam, beginning at the fold. *Backstitch (p. 19)* a few stitches at the beginning, and **PIVOT** 1/2" (1.3 cm) from the corner. Backstitch a few stitches at the end. *Trim the seam allowances diagonally (p. 51)* at the corner where you pivoted.

11 Set the machine for a **ZIGZAG STITCH** of medium length (2.5 mm) and near maximum width (4 mm). Finish the edges of the seam allowances by stitching so that the right-hand stitches go just over the edges and the left-hand stitches go into the fabric. Turn the pillow case right side out, and give it a final pressing.

Flanged PILLOW SHAMS

FLANGED shams transform ordinary bed pillows into custom designer pillows. Because there are few measurements to take and the straight **SEAMS** and **HEMS** are easy to sew, a sham is a good beginning sewing project. Flanged shams can be made to fit standard-size, queen-size, or king-size pillows. An overlapping closure in the center of the back makes it easy to insert and remove the pillow. Select decorator fabric to coordinate with your duvet or bedspread.

WHAT YOU'LL LEARN

How to PIVOT the stitching line to make perfect square corners

How to guide your stitching line at a depth beyond the seam allowance guides

How to make a flange

How to make a lapped opening

WHAT YOU'LL NEED

1⅝ yd. (1.5 m) of 54" (137 cm) decorator fabric for each pillow sham

Thread

Masking tape

How to Sew a PILLOW SHAM

1

PILLOW SIZE	CUT SIZE OF FRONT	CUT SIZE OF EACH BACK
Standard 20" × 26" (51 × 66 cm)	27" × 33" (68.5 × 84 cm)	27" × 19" (68.5 × 48.5 cm)
Queen 20" × 30" (51 × 76 cm)	27" × 37" (68.5 × 94 cm)	27" × 21" (68.5 × 53.5 cm)
King 20" × 36" (51 × 91.5 cm)	27" × 43" (68.5 × 109 cm)	27" × 24" (68.5 × 61 cm)

LET'S BEGIN

1 Cut a sham front and two sham back pieces according to the measurements given in the chart.

TIP Make tissue paper patterns of the pieces for easier cutting. If your fabric has a large design or stripes, you can see through the tissue paper to center the design on the sham front piece.

2 PRESS under 1" (2.5 cm) on one long edge of a back piece. Unfold the pressed edge and fold the cut edge in, aligning it to the first fold line; press the outer fold.

3 Refold the hem along the pressed foldlines, encasing the raw edge to form a ¹/₂" (1.3 cm) *double-fold hem (p. 45)*. Pin the hem, *inserting the pins perpendicular to the folds (p. 19)*.

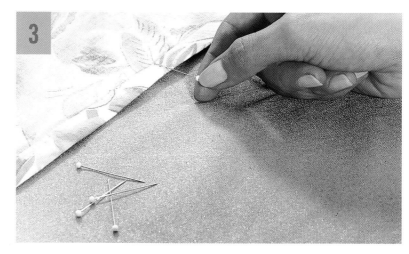

4 Set the machine for a straight stitch of 10 stitches per inch which equals 2.5 mm. Place the hem under the presser foot with the wrong side of the fabric up. Align the needle to enter the fabric just inside the inner fold. *Edgestitch (p. 92)* along the inner folded edge, *removing the pins as you come to them (p.19)*.

5 Repeat steps 2 to 4 for one long edge of the other back piece. Place the sham back pieces over the sham front, right sides together, aligning the cut edges and overlapping the back hemmed edges 3" (7.5 cm). Pin the layers together around the outer edge.

TIP Pin the layers together along the back opening using safety pins. This will keep the overlapped edges in place while you sew.

6 Mark pencil dots ¹/2" (1.3 cm) from the edges in each corner. Beginning anywhere along the outer edge, place the fabric under the presser foot, aligning the cut edges to the ¹/2" (1.3 cm) *seam allowance guide (p. 19)*. Stitch forward until you come to the dot at the first corner.

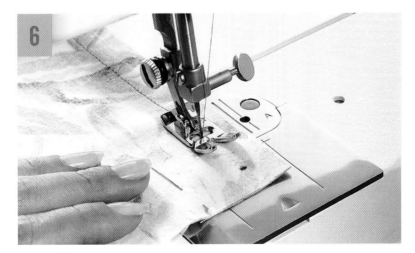

CONTINUED

How to Sew a PILLOW SHAM

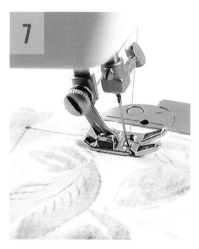

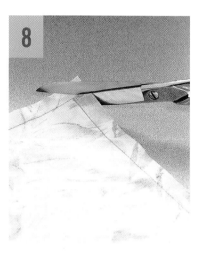

CONTINUED
----

7 Stop the machine with the needle completely down in the fabric at the dot; lift the presser foot and turn the fabric so the next side aligns to the 1/2" (1.3 cm) seam guide. Lower the presser foot and continue stitching around all four sides, pivoting in this manner at each corner. Overlap the stitches 1/2" (1.3 cm) where they meet.

8 *Remove the fabric from the machine (p. 19)* and trim the threads close to the fabric. Press the outer edges flat to set the stitches in the seam. *Trim the seam allowances diagonally (p. 51)* at the four corners to remove excess bulk.

9 Insert a heavy cardboard tube or a seam roll (page 24) into the opening and place it under the seam. Press the seam allowances open, applying light pressure with the tip of the iron down the crease of the seam.

10 Turn the pillow sham right side out, reaching in through the overlap to pull out each corner. Insert a point turner or similar tool into the sham, gently pushing the points out to form *perfect corners (p. 51).*

💡

QUICK REFERENCE

Place a piece of masking tape on the bed of your machine. Whenever you want to sew a straight seam at a depth beyond the marked seam allowance guides on the throat plate, this method is handy. Use masking tape that can be easily removed.

11 Press the seamed edges lightly, centering the seamline around the outer edge. With the front facing up, pin the layers together about 3" (7.5 cm) from the four sides, inserting the pins perpendicular to the edges.

TIP Tape the back overlapped edges closed in the area of the outer flange. You can remove the tape after stitching.

12 Mark small dots 3" (7.5 cm) from the corners of the shams to help you know when to pivot. *Place a piece of masking tape on the bed of your machine* 3" (7.5 cm) to the right of the needle, parallel to the seam allowance guide.

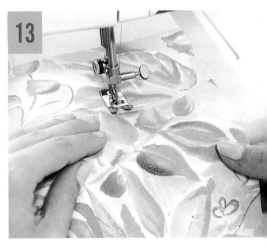

TIP Instead of watching your needle, watch the tape edge to ensure a straight stitching line. When you pivot at the dots, the next edge should align to the tape.

13 Stitch the pillow sham flange, guiding the seamed edge along the tape. Remove the pins as you come to them. Stop stitching with the needle down to pivot at each corner. Overlap the stitches 1/2" (1.3 cm) where they meet.

Duvet COVER

A duvet cover keeps a duvet or comforter clean and is easily removed for laundering. The sewing steps are fairly simple; the difficulty comes in handling large expanses of fabric. Set up a card table next to your sewing machine station to help with the task.

Duvet covers usually require two or more widths of fabric sewn together for the front and back: one full width down the center with equal partial widths along the sides. Choose a lightweight, firmly woven, washable fabric. Be aware that fabrics with large **PATTERN REPEATS** could result in a lot of wasted fabric.

WHAT YOU'LL LEARN

How to match a pattern when using more than one width of decorator fabric in a project

How to make a lapped button closure

How to sew a buttonhole

WHAT YOU'LL NEED

Fabric for top and underside of duvet cover, amount determined in step 1

Thread

Buttons, 1/2" to 5/8" (1.3 to 1.5 cm) diameter

Twill tape (page 27)

Four small plastic rings

How to Sew a DUVET COVER

1

FINISHED LENGTH of the duvet cover		86" (218.5 cm)
Add 1" (2.5 cm) for seam allowances	+	1" (2.5 cm)
to find the cut length of the front	=	87" (221 cm)
Finished length of the duvet cover		86" (218.5 cm)
Add 8½" (21.8 cm)	+	8½" (21.8 cm)
to find the cut length of the back	=	94½" (240 cm)
FINISHED WIDTH of the duvet cover		86" (218.5 cm)
Add 1" (2.5 cm) for seam allowances	+	1" (2.5 cm)
to find the cut width of the cover	=	87" (221 cm)
Divide the cut width		87" (221 cm)
by the fabric width	÷	54" (137 cm)
Round up to the next whole number		1.6
to find the number of widths needed		2
Multiply the number of widths		2
by the cut length of the front	×	87" (221 cm)
to find the amount needed for the front	=	174" (442 cm)
Multiply the number of widths		2
by the cut length of the back	×	94½" (240 cm)
to find the amount needed for the back	=	189" (480 cm)
Add the amount needed for the front		174" (442 cm)
to the amount needed for the back	+	189" (480 cm)
to find the total amount needed	=	363" (922 cm)
Convert to yards (meters); round up		=10⅛ yd. (9.25 m)

If you buy a fabric with a pattern repeat, the cut lengths must be rounded up
to the next number evenly divisible by the pattern repeat length. In our example, if
the repeat length is 7" (18 cm) the cut lengths are 91" and 98" (231 and 249 cm)
instead of 87" and 94½" (221 and 240 cm). Proceed with your figures using the
revised cut lengths.

LET'S BEGIN

1 Measure your duvet or comforter to determine the *finished size* of the cover. Use this formula to determine the **CUT LENGTH** and **CUT WIDTH** of the pieces and the amount of fabric you will need. We are using numbers for a queen-size duvet cover; yours may be different.

2 Prepare your fabric (page 33). *Measure and mark the location of each cut* along the **SELVAGE**. Cut the pieces, following the cutting guidelines (pages 34 and 35). If you do not have to match a pattern (page 36), cut away the selvages, cutting just beyond the tightly woven area. Cut one front and one back piece in half lengthwise.

3 Pin a half-width piece to the full-width front piece, right sides together, along the lengthwise edges, *inserting the pins perpendicular to the edges (p. 19)*. Match the pattern, if necessary, following the guidelines on page 36. Place the pinned edges under the presser foot with the edges aligned to the ½" (1.3 cm) *seam allowance guide (p. 19)*. The bulk of the fabric is to the left of the machine.

2
FRONT   BACK

| HALF WIDTH | FULL WIDTH | HALF WIDTH | HALF WIDTH | FULL WIDTH | HALF WIDTH |

3

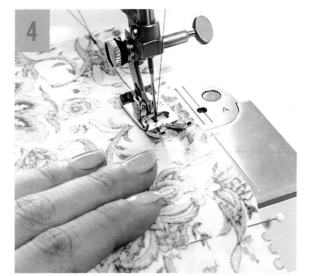

4

5

4 Set the machine for a straight stitch with 10 to 12 stitches per inch, which equals 2 to 2.5 mm. Stitch a ½" (1.3 cm) **SEAM**, *removing the pins as you come to them (p. 19). Backstitch (p. 19)* at the beginning and end of the seam.

5 Stitch the second half-width piece to the opposite side of the full-width piece, following steps 3 and 4. Set the machine for a wide **ZIGZAG STITCH** with a length of 10 stitches per inch, which equals 2.5 mm. Stitch close to the edge of each **SEAM ALLOWANCE** so that the right-hand stitches go just over the edge. This step, called a seam finish, keeps the edges from raveling.

CONTINUED

QUICK REFERENCE

Finished size. The finished size of the cover is usually the same size as the duvet measurements. For a snug fit over a down comforter, the cover may be up to 2" (5 cm) shorter and narrower than the comforter.

Measure and mark the location of each cut. Use pins or pencil marks on the selvage to mark off all the cut lengths of the pieces. Double-check your measurements before you begin cutting to avoid costly mistakes.

How to Sew a DUVET COVER

CONTINUED

---

6 **PRESS** over the stitching line of the closed seams; then open the seam allowances and press them again. Measure and cut the duvet front to the exact cut width, as determined in the chart on page 162.

TIP It may be easier to fold the pieced top in half lengthwise and measure one-half the width plus ½" (1.3 cm) from the fold line. Remember the partial widths on the sides should be equal.

7 Repeat steps 3 to 6 for the duvet cover back. Mark a line 12" (30.5 cm) from the lower edge of the back. Cut on the marked line.

8 Press under 3" (7.5 cm) along the upper edge of the small back piece. Unfold and turn the cut edge in, aligning it to the first fold line. Press outer fold.

9 Refold on the first fold line encasing the raw edge to form a 1½" (3.8 cm) *double-fold hem (p. 45)*. Pin the hem in place, inserting the pins perpendicular to the folds. *Edgestitch (p. 92)* along the inner fold line. (Remember to set the machine back to a straight stitch.)

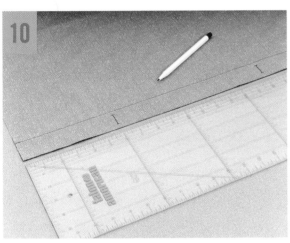

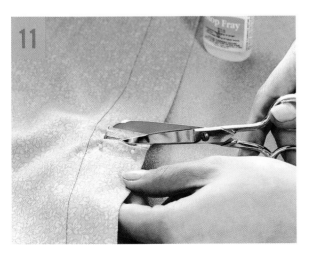

10 Press and stitch 1½" (3.8 cm) double-fold hem on the lower edge of the large back piece. Mark the placement and *length for buttonholes* on the hem of the large back piece, centered between the fold and stitching line. Place outer marks 6" (15 cm) from each side and the others spaced about 10" to 12" (25.5 to 30.5 cm) apart. Run the marks perpendicular to the hem edge.

11 Attach your buttonhole presser foot or buttonhole attachment. Follow the instructions in your owner's manual to sew buttonholes over the marked lines. Apply liquid fray preventer (page 25) to the buttonholes; allow to dry and then cut the buttonholes open.

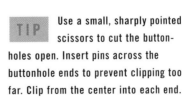

TIP Use a small, sharply pointed scissors to cut the buttonholes open. Insert pins across the buttonhole ends to prevent clipping too far. Clip from the center into each end.

CONTINUED

CONTINUED

----

12 Overlap the hemlines of the back pieces 1½" (3.8 cm), and pin them together at the outer edges. Mark the placement for the buttons on the hemline of the small back piece. Sew buttons over the marks, following the steps on page 39.

13 Button the back pieces together; place the duvet cover back over the front, right sides together, aligning the outer edges. Pin the layers together, inserting the pins perpendicular to the edges. Mark dots ½" (1.3 cm) from each corner.

14 Fold a 20" (51 cm) piece of twill tape (page 27) in half. Align the folded edge to the outer edge of the duvet cover ½" (1.3 cm) from each corner, and pin in place.

15 Stitch a ½" (1.3 cm) seam around the edge of the duvet cover, **PIVOTING** at each corner and catching the folded end of the twill tape in the stitching. Overlap the stitches ½" (1.3 cm) where they meet.

16 *Remove the fabric from the machine (p. 19)* and trim the threads close to the fabric. Press the outer edges flat to set the stitches in the seam. *Trim the seam allowances diagonally (p. 51)* at the four corners to remove excess bulk. Avoid cutting through the twill tape.

17 Unbutton the opening. Insert a heavy cardboard tube or a seam roll (page 24) into the opening and place it under the seam. Press the seam allowances open, applying light pressure with the tip of the iron down the crease of the seam.

18 Hand-stitch a plastic ring at each corner of your duvet or comforter. Spread the duvet or comforter out over your new duvet cover and tie the twill tape to the rings at each corner. Now turn the duvet cover right side out, encasing the duvet or comforter inside.

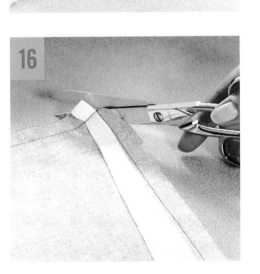

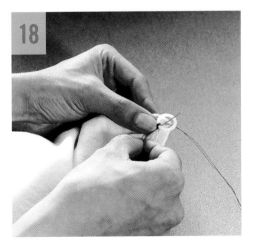

Shower CURTAIN

An easy-to-sew bathroom shower curtain adds a decorator touch. You can choose fabric to coordinate with your fixtures, tile color, and window treatment fabric. Grommets attached along the upper hem align to the grommets in a standard shower curtain liner. The **FRENCH SEAM** gives the curtain a neat appearance from both sides and keeps raw edges hidden. To make the shower curtain washable, select a washable fabric and preshrink it before you cut it.

WHAT YOU'LL LEARN

How to sew a French seam

How to sew double-fold hems

How to minimize bulk in multiple fabric layers

How to install grommets

WHAT YOU'LL NEED

4⅝ yd. (4.25 m) fabric

Water-soluble fabric marker

Twelve grommets, size 0 or ¼" (6 mm), and attaching tool

Thread to match the fabric

How to Sew a SHOWER CURTAIN

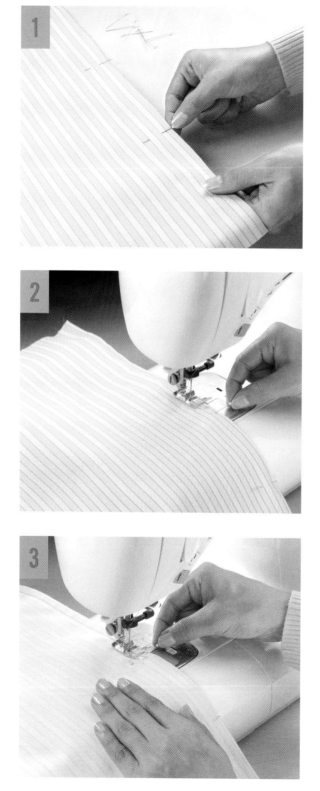

LET'S BEGIN

1 Preshrink the fabric (page 33). Cut two full-width pieces 82" (208.5 cm) long, following the cutting guidelines on page 34. Cut away the **SELVAGES** evenly, cutting just beyond the tightly woven area. Pin two vertical edges, wrong sides together, *inserting the pins perpendicular to the edges (p. 19).*

2 Place the fabric under the presser foot, aligning the raw edges to the ¼" *(6 mm) seam allowance guide.* Stitch ¼" (6 mm) **SEAM**, *backstitching (p. 19)* at the beginning and end of the seam. *Remove the pins as you come to them (p. 19). Remove the fabric from the machine (p. 19).*

3 **PRESS** the seam allowances to one side. Then fold the fabric, right sides together, with the seam exactly on the fold; press. Pin, inserting the pins perpendicular to the fold. Stitch again, guiding the folded edge along the ⅜" (1 cm) seam allowance guide, and removing the pins as you come to them. This encases the raw edges in what is known as a French seam. Press the seam allowances to one side.

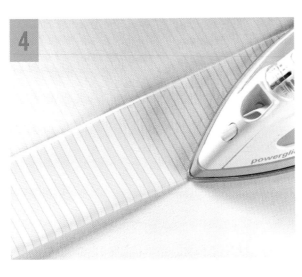

4 Cut one vertical edge of the shower curtain so the total width is 76" (193 cm). The finished width of a standard shower curtain is 72" (183 cm). This allows 2" (5 cm) on each side for hemming. Place the curtain facedown on a pressing surface. *Press under (p. 45)* the lower edge 6" (15 cm) for the hem. Unfold the pressed edge. Turn the cut edge back, aligning it to the pressed foldline; press the outer fold.

5 Refold the hem along the pressed foldlines, encasing the raw edge to form a 3" (7.5 cm) *double-fold hem (p. 45)*. Pin the hem, inserting the pins perpendicular to the foldlines.

6 Stitch the hem, guiding the presser foot along the inner fold of the hem. Backstitch a few stitches at the beginning and end. Remove pins as you come to them.

CONTINUED

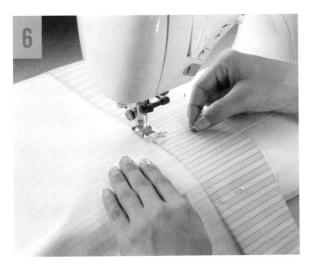

QUICK REFERENCE

1/4" (6 mm) seam allowance guide. The seam allowance guide on the throat plate may not have a line for 1/4" (6 mm). On some machines, the distance from the tip of the needle to the right edge of the presser foot measures exactly 1/4" (6 mm). If this is not true of your machine, mark a 1/4" (6 mm) seam guide on the bed of the machine with tape.

How to Sew a SHOWER CURTAIN

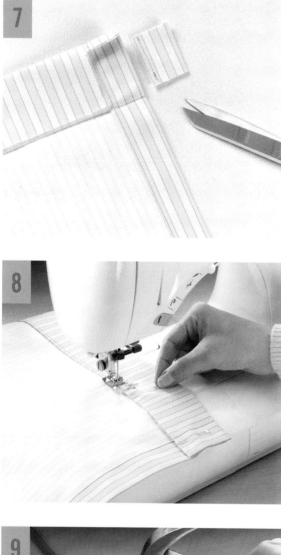

7 Repeat steps 4 to 6 for the side hems, pressing under 2" (5 cm) first, instead of 6" (15 cm). Follow step 4 for the top hem, pressing under 4" (10 cm) first. Unfold the fabric at the corners. *Trim out the excess fabric* from the inner layer, as shown, trimming to within 3/8" (1 cm) of the fold.

8 Refold the upper edge, and pin. Stitch along the inner fold, backstitching a few stitches at the beginning and end. Remove pins as you come to them.

9 Mark the placement for 12 evenly spaced grommets along the upper hem, using a fabric marker. Position them 3/4" (2 cm) from the upper edge with the outer marks centered in the side hems. Read the manufacturer's directions for attaching the grommets, and test the technique on a sample of fabric folded several times. Attach the grommets.

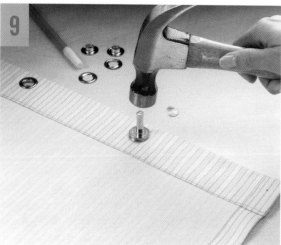

QUICK REFERENCE

Trim out the excess fabric. Eliminating some of the bulk from this area will make it easier to install the end grommets. The cutting tool will have to go through six layers of fabric instead of nine.

MORE IDEAS

Make a coordinating valance for your
shower curtain, following the directions for a
self-lined rectangle valance on page 46.
Plan the valance to have a finished width of
72" (18 cm) and a finished length of
10" (25.5 cm). Instead of grommets, stitch
buttonholes along the upper hem of the shower
curtain and the upper edge of the valance.

APPLIQUÉ. This French word refers to a decoration or cutout that is applied to the surface of a larger piece of fabric. Many methods of appliqué are used, including simply machine stitching around the outline of the decoration.

BASTE. Long, easy-to-remove, straight stitches are sewn into the fabric temporarily, either by hand or by machine.

BIAS refers to the diagonal direction of a piece of fabric. True bias is at a 45-degree angle to both the lengthwise and crosswise grains. Woven fabric has considerable stretch on the bias.

CASING. A fabric tunnel, through which something will be inserted, is sewn into an item. One example is the rod pocket at the top of a curtain panel. A casing can also hold a drawstring or elastic.

CROSSWISE GRAIN. On woven fabric, the crosswise grain runs perpendicular to the selvages. Fabric has slight "give" on the crosswise grain.

CUT LENGTH refers to the total length at which fabric should be cut for a project. It includes allowances for hems, seams, rod pockets and matching prints.

CUT WIDTH refers to the total width at which fabric should be cut for a project. If more than one width of fabric is needed, the cut width refers to the entire panel after seams are sewn, including allowances for any side hems or seams.

DARTS. Fabric is folded and stitched to remove excess fullness and give shape to an item. For instance, darts are sewn at the front corners of a chair seat cover to make the fabric conform to the front corners of the seat.

DIRECTIONAL PRINT. The design printed on the fabric may have definite "up" and "down" directions, such as flowers growing upward. All pieces for a project should be cut so that the print will run in the correct direction when the project is finished.

DROP LENGTH is the length of a tablecloth from the edge of the table to the edge of the cloth. It can be anywhere from 6" (15 cm) to floor-length.

FABRIC IDENTIFICATION LABEL. Found on every bolt or tube of fabric, this label informs you of the fiber content, width, and care method for the fabric. The labels on patterned decorator fabrics also indicate the length of the pattern repeat.

FLANGE is a border of flat fabric that extends beyond the stitching line around the outer edge of a pillow, pillow sham, or duvet cover.

FRENCH SEAM. Two pieces of fabric are joined together in a two-step seam that encases the raw edges. First a narrow seam is sewn with the wrong sides together. Then the fabric is refolded on the seamline and stitched again with the right sides together. This is especially useful when an item

will be seen from both sides, such as a shower curtain.

FULLNESS describes the finished width of a curtain in proportion to the length of the rod. For example, two times fullness means that the width of the curtain measures two times the length of the rod.

GRAINLINES. Woven fabrics have two grainlines, lengthwise and crosswise, which coincide with the yarns running in both directions at right angles to each other. In order for a finished project to hang or lay straight, horizontal and vertical cuts must follow the grainlines exactly.

HEM. The outer edge of a project is given a neat finished appearance by turning under and securing the raw edge in one of several methods. For home décor items, edges are often turned under twice and stitched, encasing the raw edge in a double-fold hem.

INTERLINING is a layer if fabric encased between the top fabric and the lining for the purpose of preventing light from shining through or to add body for items like window toppers or valances.

LENGTHWISE GRAIN. On woven fabric, the lengthwise grain runs parallel to the selvages. Fabrics are generally stronger along the lengthwise grain.

LINED TO THE EDGE means that a fabric panel is backed with lining that is cut to the exact same size. The two pieces are joined together by a seam around the outer edge, with the raw edges of the seam allowances concealed between the layers.

LINING is a fabric backing sewn to the top fabric that hides the underside. For window treatments, lining provides extra body, protection from sunlight, and support for side hems or seams. For items like placemats and reversible seat covers, the lining gives the item a neat finished appearance from both sides.

MITERED. Excess fabric on a corner is folded out diagonally to reduce bulk. This creates smooth, neat corner edges.

MUSLIN. This mediumweight, plainly woven, cotton fabric is relatively inexpensive, so it is often used for drafting patterns when paper isn't feasible. Unbleached muslin is off-white with tiny brown flecks; bleached muslin is white.

NOMINAL LUMBER. The actual measurement of nominal or "stock" lumber differs from the nominal size. A 1 × 2 board actually measures 3/4" × 1 1/2" (2 × 3.8 cm). Always measure boards for accuracy.

NONDIRECTIONAL PRINT. The design printed on this type of fabric has no definite "up" or "down" directions, so pieces that will be seamed together can be laid out with the top edges facing in either direction.

PATTERN REPEAT, a characteristic of decorator fabrics, is the lengthwise distance from one distinctive point in the pattern, such as the tip of a petal in a floral motif, to the exact same point in the next motif.

PIVOT. Perfect corners are stitched by stopping with the needle down in the fabric at the exact corner before turning the fabric. To be sure the corner stitch locks, turn the handwheel until the needle goes all the way down and just begins to rise.

PRESSING. This step is extremely important to the success of your sewing projects. Select the heat setting appropriate for your fabric and use steam. Lift and lower the iron in an overlapping pattern. Do not slide the iron down the seam, as this can cause the fabric to stretch out of shape, especially on the crosswise grain or bias.

RAILROADING. The lengthwise grain of the fabric is run horizontally in the project, usually to eliminate the need for any vertical seams. Some decorator fabrics are intentionally made this way, in widths that can accommodate floor-length window treatments.

SEAM. Two pieces of fabric are placed right sides together and joined near the edge with stitches. After stitching, the raw edges are hidden on the wrong side, leaving a clean, smooth line on the right side.

SEAM ALLOWANCE. Narrow excess fabric between the stitching line and the raw edge gives the seam strength and ensures that the stitches cannot be pulled off the raw edges.

SELVAGES. Characteristic of woven fabrics, these narrow, tightly woven outer edges should be cut away, or they may cause seams to pucker and may shrink excessively when laundered.

TEMPORARY FABRIC ADHESIVE. Available in a convenient spray can, this product can be used to hold two fabric pieces together temporarily until they are stitched together permanently. The adhesive is light and colorless, and will not gum up the sewing machine needle. Some brands of the adhesive simply diminish after a few weeks. Others can be removed by laundering.

THREAD JAM. No matter how conscientious you are, threads can become tangled up in a wad under the fabric and cause the machine to get "stuck." DON'T USE FORCE! Remove the presser foot, if you can. Snip all the threads you can reach from the top of the throat plate. Open the bobbin case door or throat plate, and snip away threads until you can remove the bobbin. Gently remove the fabric. Thoroughly clean out the feed dog and bobbin area before reinserting the bobbin and starting over. Then just chalk it up to experience and get over it!

ZIGZAG STITCH. In this setting, the needle alternately moves from left to right with each stitch. You can alter the width of the needle swing as well as the length between stitches. A zigzag stitch that is twice as wide as it is long gives you a balanced stitch, appropriate for finishing seam allowances.

A

Adjusting sewing
   machine tension, 16–17
Appliqué, 111, 113, 174

B

Backstitching, 19
Balancing
   thread tension, 16–17
Banded tablecloth, 87–93
Baste, 174
Basting tape, 26
Batting, 27
Beeswax for thread, 21
Bias, 30, 174
Bobbins, 11
   winding, 13
Buttons,
   covered, 28
   marking placement, 101
   sew-through, 39
   shank, 39
Buttonholes, 69
   duvet cover, 165
   length, 165
Button-tufted
   cushion, 95–103

C

Casing, curtain, 73, 174
Checkerboard
   pillow, 122–125
Clipping seam allowance, 99
Coach valance, 60
Cord-and-tassel swag, 61
Cording and tassels
   for cushions, 102
Corners, perfect, 51
Cover,
   duvet, 161–167
   seat, reversible, 105–109
Crosswise grain, 30, 174
Curtains,
   relaxed rod-pocket, 73–77
   shower, 168–173
   tent flap, 61
Cut length, 174
Cut width, 174
Cutting boards, 25
Cutting fabrics,
   decorator, 35–37
Cutting tools, 23

D

Darts, 105–109, 174
Decorator,
   fabrics, 34–35
   pillows, 135–141
Design motif,
   finding center, 107
Designs, matching, 38–39

Directional prints,
   43, 143, 152, 174
Double-fold hem, 45
Drapery weights, 76
Drop length, 8, 174
Duvet cover, 161–167

E

Edgestitching, 92, 109
Envelope pillows, 143–147
Eyelet for cushions, 103

F

Fabric
   decorator, 34
   glues, 25
   identification label, 32, 174
   preparation, 33
   shopping for, 32
   types, 30
Facing, 145
Finished size, 163
Flanged pillow
   shams, 155–159, 174
Fleece throw, 111–113
Fray preventer, 25
Fraying napkin edges, 93
French seam, 169, 174
Fusible web, 26

G

Glue, fabric, 25
Grain, fabric, 30, 97
Grainlines, 136, 174
Grommets, 26, 172

H

Half widths for curtains, 75
Hand stitches, 38
Harem pillows, 127–129
Hems, double-fold, 45, 77, 174

I

Interlining, 63, 174
Irons, 24–25

J

Jacquard pillows, 141

K

Knife-edge pillows, 115–119

L

Lengthwise grain, 30, 174
Lined-to-the-edge
   valance, 53, 174
Lining, 47, 175
Liquid fray
   preventer, 25, 101

M

Machine basting, 55
Marking tools, 22
Mat for cutting, 25, 113
Measuring, 22
Mitered corners, 87, 175
Mock box pillows, 130–133
Muslin pattern, 106–107

N

Napkins, 85, 93
Needle threader, 21

Needles,
   for hand sewing, 20
   sewing machine, 10, 12
Needlework pillow, 142
Nine-patch pillows, 123–125
Nondirectional print, 63, 175

P

Paper-backed fusible web, 26
Patch-work pillow, 123–125
Pattern repeats,
   32–37, 16, 175
Pillow,
   cases, 149–153
   decorator, 135–141
   envelope, 143–147
   forms, 29
   harem, 127–129
   jacquard, 141
   knife-edge, 114–119
   mock box, 131–133
   needlework, 142
   nine-patch, 123–125
   shams, flanged, 155–159
Pincushion, 21
Pins and needles, 20
Pins, inserting
   and removing, 19
Pivot points, 107
Pivoting, 116, 139, 166, 175
Placemats, 79–85, 93
Point turner, 24
Polyurethane foam, 29
   cutting, 97
Pompom, fabric, 113
Preshrinking fabric, 33, 175
Press cloth, 25
Presser feet, 11
Pressing, 175
   seams, 24
   tools, 22, 24
   under, 45

Q

Quilted placemats, 93

R

Railroaded
   fabric, 47, 175
Raw edges, finishing, 59
Relaxed rod-pocket
   curtains, 72–77
Reversible seat
   covers, 105–109
Ribbons and trims, 29
Rotary cutter and
   mat, 23, 113, 150–151
Ruffles for cushions, 102

S

Scarf swags, 42–45
Seam allowance, 175
   machine guide, 19, 175
   masking tape guide, 159
   trimming diagonally, 51
Seam ripper, 23
Seam roll, 24
Seams, 18–19, 175
Seat covers,
   reversible, 105–109
Self-lined rectangle
   valance, 46–51

Selvages, 30, 175
Sewing machine, 8–17
   accessories for, 11
   adjusting tension, 17
   balancing tension, 16
   bobbins, 11
   needles, 10, 12
   parts, 8–13
   presser feet, 11,
   threading, 14–15,
   winding bobbin, 13
Shams, flanged, 155–159
Shower curtain, 169–173
Slipstitch, 38, 117
Squaring off
   end of fabric, 89
Stitching over
   previous stitches, 83
Strap-tied valance, 53–61
Supplies, sewing, 20–25
Swag,
   cord-and-tassel, 61
   scarf style, 43–45
Symmetry, 97
Synthetic fleece
   throw, 111–113

T

Tablecloth, banded, 87–93
Tassels for cushions, 102
Temporary
   fabric adhesive, 112, 175
Tent flap curtains, 61
Thimble, 21
Thread, button and carpet, 28
Thread jam, 18, 54, 175
Threading,
   hand needle, 38
   sewing machine, 14–15
Tiered valance, 60
Tools,
   measuring and marking, 22
   pressing, 22
Trimming out
   excess fabric, 172
Trims and ribbons,
   29, 135–141, 147
Turning back
   seam allowance, 99
Twill tape, 27

V

Valance,
   self-lined, 47–51
   shower curtain, 173
   strap-tied, 32–61
   tiered, 60

W

Web, fusible, 26
Welting, 27, 102
Winding bobbins, 13
Window topper, 63–71

Z

Zigzag stitch, 58, 175
Zipper, 28
   foot, 11, 120
   for cushions, 103
   for pillows, 118–121, 135
   polyester coil, 28
   stops, 119